# From PROJECTS to PUBLISHER

## NAVIGATING THE CHAPTERS OF LIFE WHILE MAXIMIZING YOUR LANE

*Shenitha Finesse Anniec*

S.H.E. PUBLISHING, LLC

**From PROJECTS to PUBLISHER**

Copyright © 2024 by Shenitha Finesse Anniece

For information contact: www.shepublishingllc.com

Library of Congress Control Number: 2023952267

ISBN:
978-1-953163-86-8 (hardback)
978-1-953163-85-1 (paperback)
978-1-953163-90-5 (eBook)
978-1-964061-05-4 (audio)

First Edition: May 2024

10 9 8 7 6 5 4 3 2 1

# TRIBUTE

To the incredible authors who entrusted their stories to us, the class of 2020 to 2023, "From Projects to Publisher" is a heartfelt tribute and my expression of gratitude to you. Your courage to share your stories, your willingness to embark on this literary journey, and your belief in the power of SHE PUBLISHING LLC has been the driving force behind the birth of a passion I never knew I had.

As I write these words, they fall short in capturing the depth of appreciation and admiration for each one of you. As I often say, there would be no SHE without you, and this book is more than just ink on paper; it is a manifestation of our collective journey. Your stories have created ripples, resonating with readers across the globe, and together, we are navigating the chapters of life while maximizing our respective lanes.

So, to the trailblazers who believed in SHE, thank you for being the architects of change, for infusing vitality into this passion project, and for becoming an integral part of the SHE Publishing family. As we celebrate our stories, remember that our narratives have forever enriched the literary landscape, and our legacy continues to inspire countless others to share their voices.

With gratitude,

Shenitha Finesse Anniece, CEO and Founder of
SHE PUBLISHING LLC

# ACKNOWLEDGMENTS

In humble acknowledgment, I express gratitude to Him for the guidance, inspiration, and grace bestowed upon me throughout the journey of writing this book. It is with reverence and awe that I recognize the hand of God in every word written, every idea conceived, and every insight gained. May His presence continue to light the path ahead, infusing these pages with wisdom for all who journey through them.

I would like to express my heartfelt gratitude to the pioneering publishing companies that laid the foundation for the thriving world of literature, with a special nod to the very first printing press that paved the way for all those that followed, which was invented in Germany in the mid-15th century, from what I researched. From what I researched, the first book publishers were Schwabe Verlag in Switzerland, the House of Elzevir, and the Cambridge University Press2. The Cambridge University Press, founded by Henry VIII in 1534, released the first print book in 1582.

To my esteemed Publishing Friends, and sister publishing companies, your camaraderie, shared insights, and support have been invaluable on this literary journey. Together, we've strengthened the bonds of the publishing industry.

A huge thank you goes out to my parents, whose unconditional love, encouragement, and sacrifices have been the bedrock of my personal and professional growth. Your belief in my dreams has fueled my determination, and I am forever grateful for the lessons you've instilled in me.

To my immediate family (*Jada, Jasmyn, Jordyn, Jade, Jermaine, Janisha & Jrogo*), you are my pillars of strength, my constant cheerleaders. Your support and understanding have been the driving force behind the establishment and success of SHE PUBLISHING LLC. I am blessed to have you by my side.

To my Federal Judiciary Family, I extend my appreciation. You have been a community that has been an integral part of my life's journey from childhood to adulthood. The invaluable experiences, lessons, my best friends at work, leadership experience and mentee/mentorship provided by this remarkable organization has played a pivotal role in shaping me both professionally and personally.

To my beloved Toastmasters family, your support and uplifting atmosphere have also been instrumental in fostering my personal and professional growth. Through your encouragement, I have cultivated invaluable skills in relationship building, leadership, self-confidence, and career advancement. I am deeply grateful for the opportunities to refine my abilities in facilitating effective and productive meetings, honing my leadership abilities, and serving others with greater empathy and understanding. Your guidance has significantly elevated my performance across all facets of my life, and for that, I am thankful.

Finally, I want to express my heartfelt acknowledgment to my uncle Eric, whose inspiration and encouragement sparked the creation of this project. Without your influence, I would have never even considered such an endeavor. Our humble beginnings have laid the groundwork for this passion project. I am truly thankful for the opportunities in my life that have allowed me to achieve such a remarkable milestone.

The legacy of the pioneering publishing companies, the camaraderie of Publishing Friends, my Federal Judiciary Family, Toastmasters Family, and the boundless love from my parents and immediate family have collectively shaped my journey. I extend my deepest gratitude to all, for you are the roots that anchor me and the wings that lift me. I love you all to pieces, and I mean it.

Sincerely,

Shenitha Finesse Anniece

# FOREWORD

As I write this foreword, first and foremost, I would like to thank God for blessing me with the most precious gift, my daughter, Shenitha "Finesse" Anniece. She has and continues to make me proud, and I want to thank her for keeping me in her "Playground." She has always, since an early age, looked at life as a big playground – not only that, but she also plays hard!

In raising Shenitha, I noticed that she always focused on the goodness of people. She not only loves people, but she loves life, family, and her yearning for valued friendships. Shenitha is a servant leader – always putting one's needs before her own. Family traditions are of the utmost importance to Shenitha! According to her, *"You have to Live a Little!"* Her creativity, bravery, capability, and passion for entrepreneurship began at the early age of nine (9).

Shenitha strongly believes that everyone has a story to tell that they should share with the world. Leaving your legacy behind, which will be very impactful, is so very important to her. Because S.H.E.nitha wanted to share her personal story with her four (4) daughters, S.H.E. Publishing LLC was born!

Shenitha's decision to write *"From Projects to Publisher,"* makes my heart happy and I hope it will do the same for all her readers. Even though the projects are no longer, the experiences and memories will never ever die! Thank you, baby, for sharing your story!

Growing up in the "Jets," that is what we called the projects back in the day, and giving birth to my one and only child was very challenging yet lots of fun! We faced hard times, continued to play hard and safe, and because of that, this created an opportunity for the world to read this amazing story.

To my Baby, my ACE, I am so very proud of you. I love your resilience, your determination, and your strength to keep moving forward. Your genuine love for the betterment of others to help make their dreams come true is mind blowing! I will always, as long as I live, be a part of the "Playground" you call Life! You ROCK! Keep up the fine job!

I'm so very happy that God connected us as Mother and Daughter!

Love Eternally!

Mommy

# TESTIMONIALS

*"Shenitha's vision and passion are evident when you are in her presence. The ability to see something she wants and go after it is what made me want to collaborate with her. I truly believe Shenitha can and will accomplish all she puts her mind to!"*
**--Jon Ross, Emmy Nominated Film Producer**

*"S.H.E. Publishing LLC is not just a publisher, it's a family - a family of writers, editors, designers, and readers. They bring a profound sense of commitment to their work, nurturing each author's vision with care, respect, and an unwavering belief in the power of words. It's much more than just a business relationship: it's about creating an extra special atmosphere. Every interaction with them is enveloped in their innate warmth and understanding, making what can often be a daunting process, a remarkably enjoyable journey. They are not only passionate about what they do, but also about who they do it for: the authors and the readers. Working with them has been an amazing experience, one that I will never forget. I'm grateful for the opportunity to see my dream finally realized and I wholeheartedly recommend S.H.E. Publishing LLC to any author who seeks a publisher who truly values their craft and would like to also see their own dreams come to life."*
**--Dr. Samuel I. Brown, Author of Wounds Can Heal**

*"Working with SHENITHA as my publisher has been an absolute delight. Her unparalleled dedication and warm, familial approach make the publishing journey not just professional but truly personal. If you are willing to put in the work, she will*

*help make your dreams come true."*
**--Richnovated, Author of E.N.G.I.N.RE.E.R. Your Way**

*"This is an awesome publishing company. When I wrote my first book, I self-published, and I learned the hard way about all the work and professionalism required to successfully publish a project. When I went to SHE Publishing for the second book, they knew the processes and procedures to get my book where it needed to be in the time that it needed to be there. They took care of everything, and I have experienced nothing but professionalism. They really care about their authors and want every project to achieve success. They worked extremely hard promoting my project and got it released in a very timely manner. After self-publishing my first book, I was very pleased with the editing and layout modifications that we incorporated into the manuscript. It made my work appear as if it were prepared for kings! I wrote this review with my book in pre-release mode,
and already it is number one in its category on \*\*\*\*\*\*.
I highly recommend SHE Publishing!*
**--Pastor Henry L. Razor, Award-Winning Author of Your Purpose is Your Superpower**

*"Yesterday's Holiday -Views live was crazy! It was probably one of the more lively virtual roundtables that I've been a part of more so than any other! We spoke about our upcoming projects and talked about our favorite movies and I finally shared the history behind my Black Cyrano name and brand, which I had never divulged to ANYONE until last night! If you missed yesterday's live, go visit the @she.publishing.llc YouTube page and watch it! I love my #shefamily!"*
**--Marc A. Beausejour, Author of the BlackCyrano Series**

*SHE PUBLISHING LLC is founded and led by the fearless, loving, incredible Shenitha Burton who has created an incredible community for black authors and now for young authors. Finally, my daughter is a founding member of The Little She Project. 2024 has miracles waiting.*
**--B_LIST_LIVING**

*To my new family, it was simply amazing to be a part of such an incredible organization | SHE. I am so looking forward to becoming a true inspiration and product of the family. I felt lots of love, so I know I definitely made the right decision with connecting with the SHE Family.*
**--Latoya Johnson, Author of The Beauty Beneath the Queen OF MASSAGE THERAPY: Unmasking the Realities of Lipo/360, Tummy Tucks, and BBL Fairytales."**

*S.H.E. Publishing, LLC is a company that genuinely values the importance of familial bonds. My first interaction with the founder and CEO, was nothing short of remarkable. From the moment we started talking, it felt like we had known each other for years. Our conversation lasted over an hour, and by the end of it, I was convinced that I had found the perfect partner for my business endeavors. Over the past year, our relationship has only grown stronger, and our shared passion for excellence has led us to form a dynamic partnership that promises to be mutually beneficial.*
**--Dr. Calenthia Miller, Author of UNMASK and CEO of A'Lure Publishing LLC**

*I was very pleased with the hands-on service I received from S.H.E. Publishing. With this being my 1st book, I had so many questions & concerns and at no point did they make me feel like I*

*was a bother. My phone calls & emails were answered in a timely manner. My plan is to make my book into a series. I'm looking forward to continuing my business with them. Other people have asked me how did I do it. My answer is with the help from S.H.E. Publishing. They took a lot of stress off me, not really knowing where to start. Ill recommend them to everyone that ask, and I pray for their Big Success to continue! Because of S.H.E. Publishing, I can now add Author to my resume! Thanks for Everything! Author of Martell's World You're No Different Than Me.*
**—Cynthia Green, Author of Martell's World**

*S.H.E. Publishing, LLC has provided me with what I needed to get my book Published and through them I am able to get other books published. They were friendly, thorough, and patient, walking me through the process. I am pleased with the project, and I look forward to doing more business with S.H.E*
**--Pamela Fields, Author of HER Poetry Book Series**

*Normally, I always say, "Do your own stuff!" However, having a team to sincerely cheer you on! I absolutely loved being with SHE PUBLISHING LLC this weekend. The love!!! The support! The family!! If you are on a journey of wanting to start but don't want to start alone, Shenitha will make sure you are taken care of for real!*
**--BlackMomsReality_b.c**

*As a writer when I think of SHE PUBLISHING LLC the first word that comes to mind is EXCELLENCE! Everything that She Publishing does is done in excellence from the outset and it is consistent, tailored for each author. I have recently been honored to receive an award from the Black Authors Matter organization for an interview I did on Jan 9, 2024. Thanks to Shenitha and the She Publishing family, I was able to attend the National Black Book Festival in Houston Tx. She Publishing is always looking to grow all the Authors on the roster. From one-on-one conversations, or holding a zoom class, SHE is always working on our behalf. I feel blessed and honored to be a part of the SHE family.*

**—Royce Dixon, Author of Hidden Feelings Revealed**

*I joined S.H.E. Publishing LLC back in November 2023 and it turned out to be the best decision that I've made in my literary career. Prior to joining S.H.E. I was contracted with a privately owned publishing company that did not promote or market my novels to my core audience and readers. As a result I would see very little results in terms of monthly sales. If I am not promoting my books or going to book fairs, my book series would not gain any serious traction. I was seriously considering ending my career as an author because I felt defeated and although I've made financial sacrifices to advance my career, I would see no ascension in my journey. But my concerns ended once I joined S.H.E. Publishing. The C.E.O. was very personable, and she was very timely with her responses via email and text. If my books were being published, she always provided me with a time frame of when the books would be distributed through retailers and each deadline was met, down to the letter! I am thoroughly pleased with the services they provide, and they've helped relaunch my book series and also published and released a new novel in the series all within a 2-month span. I also love the fact that we hold Zoom meetings to discuss book tours which helps with planning and preparation. I've never been part of a literary family, so when I met the other authors of S.H.E., they made me feel like I was a part of their family from the very first day I met them. I love my*

*brothers and sisters in authorship and I'm looking forward to taking another leap in this journey while representing my S.H.E. family!*
—**Marc A Beausejour, Author of the BlackCyrano Series**

# PREFACE

*From Projects to Publisher* diggs into the art of manifesting dreams, drawing inspiration from the blueprints of others while forging a unique path. Have you ever experienced an "ah-hah" moment when someone shares their story? Suddenly, you realize your life isn't as bleak as it seems, or perhaps your current situation is a result of your own actions. Indeed, you come to understand that you are precisely where you need to be.

The aim of this narrative is to ignite a spark within you—to encourage you to make the decision to stay or leave that job, embark on that journey, and splurge on yourself. If you're living paycheck to paycheck, take solace in the fact that you're not alone. Many others share this struggle. It's time to invest in yourself—to prioritize your own growth and well-being. *It's time to live a little.*

I don't dwell too much on the decisions I make in life, but that doesn't mean I don't consider the opportune risks. They say overthinking leads to paralysis. I understand the importance of weighing the options, but ultimately, I trust my instincts. When I decide to pursue something, I know it could go either way—success or me falling forward, which means that every step, regardless of the outcome, brings us all closer to our aspirations.

Throughout my journey of life, I've always infused the positions I've held with my unique strengths. Reacting and adapting have been key components of every position I've held. Just because you're trained for a job doesn't mean you can't add your personal touch to it. People remember and value your individual approach. I used to joke with my mother, saying, "I acted my way up today," meaning I dove into tasks without a clear roadmap, simply figuring it out as I went along.

One instance stands out: when my boss tasked me with drafting a proposal and organizing a leadership retreat for the leaders of our organization. This was not a duty on my job description—I guess you can say it was other duties as assigned, and I definitely hadn't been trained for it…, but I accepted the challenge. I did the research via Google, reviewed sample forms, and reached out to the listed instructors to plan relevant leadership sessions. I made it work. As a matter of fact, my team of leaders collectively contributed to our travels, tours, and crafting our extracurricular learning activities.

Another memorable occasion was when my Toastmasters' team and I were responsible for orchestrating a training session for over 100 people in our district. We'd lost the designated meeting space. So what did we do? We decided to move the training to a lunchroom on short notice. In just a few hours, our team pooled tangible and financial resources, arranged catering, and executed the event seamlessly, without anyone realizing the last-minute scramble. It was a testament to our ability to adapt and thrive under pressure.

On another note, and to flip the script, this book is also a call for more transparency, for open communication, and for a shift in the power dynamics within the publishing world. Authors deserve more than boilerplate contracts and generic advice; they deserve a family, partners, champions, and allies who understand the intricacies of their craft and the vulnerabilities that come with baring their souls on paper. The change, I believe, needs to go beyond individual transactions. We need to foster a more supportive community, where publishers and authors collaborate, where knowledge is shared freely, and where success is celebrated not just by the few, but by the entire tribe.

I yearn for a future where authors are empowered to make informed decisions, where publishers act as guides and not seen as gatekeepers, and where stories, in all their diverse forms, find their way into the hands of readers eager to be transported, inspired, and transformed.

This is the legacy I hope to leave behind: a legacy of transparency, collaboration, and shared success. This is my exit plan, not from the industry I love, but towards a future where my confessions become a catalyst for positive change, a testament to the power of storytelling, and a reminder that every voice, and every dream, deserves to be heard.

Overall, this story is about sharing my approach and experiences, in the hopes of inspiring you to persevere in the upcoming year and beyond. I draw inspiration from the stories of remarkable individuals at SHE Publishing LLC, and it's my privilege to compile them in this book. I encourage you to absorb these blueprints, adding them to your inspirational collection and finding those that resonate deeply with you.

# CONTENTS

# INTRODUCTION

## Dreams do Come True

*"Visualize this thing you want. See it, feel it, believe in it. Make your mental blueprint and begin."*
**– Robert Collier**

While playing the board game of LIFE with my immediate family one Saturday evening, the cards I was dealt landed me in a private villa, I was a teacher who collected exotic fish, our family had assembled a band, and I traveled back and forth, to and from, Paris and Chicago. This game of LIFE wasn't far from my reality. I've built and own a couple of homes, I have two (2) English bulldogs—*that's exotic as it gets*, I am a developer and leader within the Federal Judiciary, my immediate family consists of eight (8), and I have been able to travel the world, because my career as a publisher requires it. As a matter of fact, in real life, I've needed that free get out of jail card due to an unexpected traffic stop.

Who says the game of LIFE can't manifest into reality? If you've ever played the board game, you understand the basics: establishing a career, nurturing a family, caring for a pet, enjoying vacations, and selecting a home. However, in our household, we added a unique twist to the game—a literal spin that transformed this game into a profound life lesson. It was our tradition to gather around the table, recounting the cards we'd been dealt, and inevitably, I found myself leading the discussion.

As we made our way around the table, it was my 11-year-old daughter's turn to share her perspective on LIFE. With candor, she expressed, "I don't like the cards I've been dealt." This moment sparked a discussion and served as the inspiration for the narrative that would fill the blank pages starting this introduction.

While my response as a parent may seem predictable, the truth is, countless individuals grapple with dissatisfaction over their life circumstances every day. They carry the weight of what they perceive as burdens, struggling to find contentment. Allow me to share my journey—a testament to rising from humble beginnings, shaped by my experiences in the Robert Taylor Project homes in Chicago, Illinois. Despite the challenges, those early years served as the foundation for who I am today, guiding me through the chapters of my real-life and steering me along the only path available to me. I can confidently say that I'm exactly where I'm meant to be.

I aspire for my journey to serve as inspiration for others, encouraging them to persevere, find gratitude amidst scarcity, and embrace their journey of becoming, using their desires as a compass. The story of SHE unfolds like a graceful dance, blending dreams with reality. SHE, once an ordinary individual, transformed into a luminary—a billionaire by birth, steering the course of this now-global publishing empire. Here, the game of life transcends mere simulation; it manifests as tangible reality.

# CHAPTER 1:
## FROM CONCRETE BEGINNINGS
### *My Life Living in the Robert Taylor Projects*

*Appreciate where you are in your journey, even if it's not where you want to be.*
*Every season serves a purpose.*
**– Unknown**

The Robert Taylor Project Homes, located in the Bronzeville neighborhood on the South Side of Chicago, Illinois, operated as a public housing project from about 1962 to 2007. It was the largest public housing development in the United States, comprising 28 nearly identical high-rises arranged in a linear layout. The buildings cascading the foundation formed a horseshoe shape that cast long shadows over the playgrounds and land that were choked with weeds and greenery. The elevators were cramped and unreliable, so taking the stairs seemed like the safer option, a choice my mother and I often made. The hallways released a perpetual odor of urine at times, disguised in darkness where numerous crimes occurred. Both women and men fell victim to assaults in those corridors, though my mother and her siblings may have been targets, I've yet to hear of any successful incidents or misfortunes befalling them. My mother having five brothers and two sisters, they relied on each other for protection. Reflecting on what I know, my mother endured attempted robberies and even faced a gunpoint threat, yet she lived to recount her experiences. Meanwhile, my father and his associates were formidable defenders of their families, their actions veiled in secrecy. Despite my mother's experiences living in the projects, my dad made sure she got home safely after their outings to the skating rink. Before he had a car, he would ride the bus with her all the way to her stop, then get off and walk her into a territory he knew all too well. I've only heard some of the stories that took place, which shall remain undisclosed. My point in sharing these times is that survival in the projects demands readiness; it's a world where you either prevail or become a casualty.

My family initially resided in apartment 1605 on the sixteenth floor of the red brick Buildings, 4101 South Federal to be exact. Later, we relocated to apartment 901 on the ninth floor within the same building. Each of my uncles and aunties with their individual families huddled in their allotted rooms. It was a city within a city, a universe compressed into four walls.

Reflecting now, it's evident that our apartment was more than just a physical structure; it encapsulated the true essence of family value, familial bonds, and the significance of cherishing shared moments. Despite not always having, we always had each other. And *having not* fostered my creativity, shaping my perspective on life and its possibilities.

For some reason, as a little girl, I've always had big aspirations. I believe I've always had a business-oriented mindset. I recall my mother secretly recording my cousins and I on a cassette tape. I was advising them to take care of their things. I was 5 years old, and my cousins were 6 & 7. There's also a vivid memory of me placing price tags on our snow-white furniture using masking tape and a black marker—I'm surprised my mom didn't put a belt to this butt. And to think about it, I even put price tags on every book I could get my hands on that was in the house. It makes me wonder; was I unknowingly being groomed to become a publisher? Was this always a part of my destiny? What I can tell you is, life as I know it would be tangled in the web of real-life writing projects and publications. My time as a child living in the projects would mold me and my experiences in publishing projects would refine me as SHEnitha, the Publisher.

While the Robert Taylor Project Homes originally meant to provide decent and affordable housing for low-income individuals, the projects devolved into a battleground within our community, plagued by gang violence, drugs, fear, crime, and the perpetuation of poverty. As I express this, I've come to understand that circumstances can unfold unexpectedly, regardless of whether you reside in the wealthiest community or in what may be classified as the tougher neighborhoods. Threats can arise from foes, friends, or even family, at any given moment.

Among the stories circulating within our family, one stands out: the tragic fate of an uncle I never had the chance to meet. Sent away from the *projects* to a supposedly safer suburban environment, he fell victim to a fatal gunshot wound to the head and died. I've also experienced the losses of another uncle to AIDS and in my early adulthood, an aunt due to complications from an outpatient surgery gone wrong.

My childhood wasn't always sunshine and smiles. I feared walking past the alleys on my way to Overton Elementary School—a school that no longer exists today. As I write, I recall being bullied by a young girl who had nothing better to occupy her time, relentless in her pursuit until I reached my breaking point and had to stand up for myself. Despite having numerous cousins I could have turned to, for reasons unknown, I never divulged the difficulties I was facing. I remember her threats of after-school confrontations, the rapid thudding of my heart as the end of the school day drew near. While she never laid a hand on me, there was an unmistakable menace in her words. If I could travel back in time to that very first day of being bullied, I would urge my younger self to confide in my parents about the ordeal and to realize that fear is universal, something everyone contends with. Despite the fear, I'd summoned courage to face the situation head-on.

As I got older, my mother and I moved to a building on Dr. Martin Luther King Jr. drive, which hummed with a melody of resilience. To live there, where the namesake of freedom echoed with every passing car, was a badge of honor I wore proudly. It was in that era during my high school years that I would meet Sharaka Leonard, the person who would give me that proclaimed name of publisher a decade plus later.

In those teenage years, I would face fear yet again, and this time I wasn't in the projects, I was staying with my father and grandmother for the summer. There would be a harrowing incident where my life was nearly threatened while walking to the store with one of my younger cousins. Passing under a viaduct, we encountered a stranger approaching us. I was caught off guard when he abruptly yanked the solid gold necklace from around my neck. Upon closer inspection of my face, he seemed to recognize me or perhaps my family, promptly returning the chain with an apology. Terrified for my safety, I rushed back to my grandmother's home, called my dad, and recounted the ordeal. I am uncertain about the events that followed, but what I can say is that the men in our family are protectors and they are from the projects.

I remember another occasion when I stayed overnight with my auntie and two of my older cousins after they moved out of the projects. The whole day felt like an adventure; I almost believed I was in a movie. I always felt safe and shielded around them; especially my aunt, she didn't play no games. My cousins looked after me because I was one of the younger cousins at that time. They made me aspire to care for our little cousins that came after me in the same way. It's gratifying to acknowledge that all of my cousins, and there are many of us, have grown into responsible and successful contributors to our communities. We've built a network of professionals within the family, which includes nurses, veterans, entrepreneurs, legal experts, talented hairstylists, construction workers, and artists to name a few. My uncles, along with one of my cousins who feels like an uncle, have fought in wars, traveled to exotic places, and met some of the most fascinating people. I hope to one day have the privilege of hearing their incredible stories. Again, my aunt, uncles, and cousins have all built successful careers. I'm immensely grateful for the supportive and accomplished family I've been fortunate to be a part of. So I must say that all of my experiences, while unique to me, resonate with countless others who have lived outside of the projects or those who've called the projects home. Whether it be the Robert Taylor Project Homes, Stateway Gardens, Dearborn Homes, Ida B. Wells, Harold Ickes Homes, or the Hilliard Homes, when you're immersed in that environment, you grow accustomed to the surroundings.

Throughout the trials and tribulations, my family remained my anchor, with my grandmothers being the steadfast pillar of support; Janice Anderson and Mable Hoskins, *may you both rest in peace.* I must also express my gratitude for my parents, who have served as my protectors and anchors throughout the uncertainties of life.

I clearly recall confiding in my mother, sharing my doubts about even reaching the age of 30. Little did I realize then that my words would place her on edge until that milestone was reached. Despite my journey commencing amidst the unforgiving concrete landscape, I refused to let my present circumstances of living in the projects dictate my future. Each scraped knee and every tear shed served as invaluable lessons etched into the fabric of my being. From these humble beginnings, a narrative blossomed, waiting to be shared— not only with the world but with myself. Like seeds planted in harsh soil, our life stories take root, eventually blooming into a testament of resilience.

Reflecting on those concrete beginnings, I am also reminded of some remarkable experiences. One that stands out is my time singing at Orchestra Hall, a place in Chicago, Illinois located on Michigan Avenue. I captivated thousands with my voice—an aspect of myself you may not have known. Participating in the All-City choir, composed of talented singers from across the Chicagoland, remains a cherished memory. I particularly enjoyed performing French pieces, stepping onto the stage in our long beautiful blue dresses and serenading the audience. Being in front of a crowd, whether it be singing or speaking, has always felt like my destiny, though its significance wasn't fully appreciated at the time.

Additionally, I was part of a singing group, affording me the opportunity to perform for those connected with well-known individuals, that was short-lived. Attending a performing arts high school, my mother, now known as "Mama*She*" ensured my involvement in extracurricular activities, allowing me to cultivate my musical talents. I learned to play the piano and saxophone, finding joy in performing classical music on the keys.

So as you turn the pages of my life becoming a publisher, hear the journey of my beginnings, the evolution of my adolescence and young adulthood, and discover how the Gemini within me permeates every facet of this story – manifesting a life lived in the shades of nature, the ink to paper that became my new love story, and acquaint yourself with the brothers and sisters in authorship who have profoundly and continue to enriched my being.

# CHAPTER 2:

## EXPLORING THE UNKNOWN

*The Birth of a Publisher*

*"The information you consume each day is the soil from which your future grows."*
**-- Unknown**

I'd say it's true that our identities are shaped by the tiny seeds sown within us, namely the experiences we encounter. The seed that started my journey toward the execution of becoming a publisher overnight commenced during the COVID-19 pandemic. Despite the adversity it brought to both me and others, it ultimately became one of the most transformative events of my life. My mother's retirement from the Federal Courts marked a significant shift, coinciding with my own accomplishment of writing a book. This transition allowed me to realize the precious moments I had been missing with my immediate family, prompting a reevaluation of my work-life balance.

Now, I delight in the simple joy of dropping off and picking up my daughters at the front door of their school—an everyday highlight that I cherish deeply. I have the opportunity to engage with my daughters during our car rides, providing encouragement for the morning when I am not disciplining them—ha ha! And at the end of the school day, I inquire about their experiences at school, particularly attentive to any signs of bullying or challenges associated with adolescence and attending a predominately white school. Additionally, I've found the freedom to indulge in preparing meals, and pursuing my passions in the evenings and on the weekends—whenever time allows. When I think about it, there have been several moments in my life that became the soil that lead me to publishing.

In chapter one, I referenced the instance where I put price tags on all of the books I could find around the house, while another significant moment was my visit to a rehabilitation facility to see my grandmother, Janice Anderson, and yet in that precise moment, I remained oblivious to the unfolding of events. I can remember sitting near her bedside and smelling her scent as her frail hand rested in mine. My grandmother, her once vibrant eyes dimmed with age and sickness, lay on the bed at the rehabilitation facility. She was a woman who held a lifetime of untold stories; stories that wanted to breathe on their own. I wanted to hear every precious memory that made her who she'd become. From what I remember being told to me, her mother was black, and her father was white, embracing a beautiful blend of cultures and backgrounds. But it would be fear that coiled around my throat as I asked her to tell me about her life. As she began to share, my voice cracked, and disrupted her with words that would strip me of ever knowing her story, "*let's wait until you get better and come home.*" This is the day I wish I could do over. This is the day that I think about every now and again, and I can't help but shed a tear.

I wanted my grandmother's laughter to fill the sterile room. I wanted her to get better and I wanted her stories to chase away the illness. But I stopped her from sharing, pushing down the yearning in my heart, content to watch her as she fell asleep. I would wait for the day she'd return home, ready to share her life, if given another moment. The reality is, I never had another opportunity, because the next time I saw my grandmother, she was in hospice, where she would draw her final breath. I didn't allow my grandmother to share her story—and instead, they were taken to the grave.

Life doesn't wait for our fears to dissipate. It churns and boils, pushing us out of our comfort zones, urging us to explore the vast unknowns within ourselves. My journey from the concrete jungle of the Robert Taylor homes to the polished floors of corporate boardrooms to becoming a publisher wasn't a straight line etched on a map. It was a host of everyday experiences, each twist and turn shaping the woman I was becoming.

Let's start with my career at McDonald's. Yes, I said it, my short-lived career with McDonald's. Its greasy scent of fries and bustling orders fueled my entrepreneurial drive, and at that time, I didn't realize it. I was taught customer service, which taught me how to interact with customers in a friendly and efficient manner. Working in a fast-paced environment like McDonald's taught me time management skills, I had to learn teamwork to ensure a smooth operation, especially during busy periods. And two additional skills were problem solving and adaptability. Again, at the time, I did not realize the valuable entrepreneurial skills that I'd learned in such a short time. McDonald's was my entrepreneurial 101 class.

While McDonald's served as a fantastic starting point, I only remained there for about six-eight months. I was offered another job opportunity at UPS that offered college credits. Despite the McDonalds manager's efforts to persuade me to stay, I knew it wasn't my long-term path, although it could have been. However, it became clear that my journey involved exploring different opportunities for growth, even if they were short-lived. The lesson I learned from this experience is that once you've absorbed the intended lesson from one opportunity, new doors will open for further learning and development—whether it be challenging or rewarding. However, it's ultimately up to us to decide whether to stay or move on. For me, it was time to move forward, and I was fortunate to have a supportive boss at McDonald's who understood my decision.

Leaving McDonald's for UPS, driven by the lure of college credit and a rebellious boyfriend, might seem like a detour, but it was there, amidst the whirring conveyor belts and late-night shifts, that my potential once more became visible to others. Their belief in me was like a whispered acknowledgment of my raw talent—a flicker that refused to be extinguished.

Now, I found myself as a truck loader for UPS, again, earning college credits along the way while I was in high school. This job taught me strategic thinking and efficiency. While packing these big semi-trucks, I had to maximize space in the truck while ensuring package integrity. Every nook and cranny had to be filled; the stores relied on my work to receive their goods undamaged. At that time,

I didn't fully grasp the significance, but every job holds meaning. Stores depend on reliable products, parents need nutritious items for their children, and we all rely on a myriad of goods, from medical supplies to clothing—packed in those trucks were our needs for daily survival. This role as a truck loader for UPS enlightened me to another dimension of the importance of serving others.

Then came the fateful day when I received a promotion at UPS. I recall driving to work with my boyfriend and his friends, particularly a memorable moment where we engaging in a spontaneous rap battle. A guy named Eric, his verse was so intense that it felt like a fusion of WuTang Clan and DMX embodied in one person. It was all camaraderie and love. Eric played a pivotal role in connecting me with my significant other.

On a side note, reminiscing about those days driving with two protective friends and my boyfriend; they were like brothers to me, and my boyfriend was becoming more than just a partner—he was becoming an indispensable friend. Looking at where I am today, in the process of launching a podcast with three men and myself, it's evident how seemingly insignificant moments like those car rides shape our lives.

Returning to that pivotal day at UPS, here I was again in the same situation I was in at McDonald's. Despite the UPS managers belief in me and their offer for me to stay, I found myself once again declining a promised role—this time, I would be declining a manager position to pursue an entry level position at the Federal Courts.

It's easy to dismiss the seemingly mundane, the jobs we take to pay the bills, the experiences we deem insignificant. But within each lies a lesson, a brushstroke adding color to our lives. Learn to wield the broom with precision, the fryer with confidence, the filing cabinet with purpose. For in mastering the small, you cultivate the skills to conquer the grand, and my grand, as I thought, my realization of a childhood prayer and dream come true! I would have a career with the Federal Judiciary.

I was a *federally* also known as a federal employee! I walked into those revolving doors, gazing up at the imposing glass facade of the federal building. Years before getting employed with the Federal Judiciary, I stood on the street where the building stood in the windy city, and I'd whispered a wish into the concrete grounds, an unspoken prayer for a place like this to work, a beacon of success in a world that often-dimmed dreams. Now, here I was, within its very walls, my steps echoing on the polished floors, a testament to the power of belief, a key that we all hold.

*"...Speak something positive into your life,"* I urge you, as I once *whispered my dream of this building into the city's heart. For within each of us lies a dormant seed, waiting for the right moment to unravel its petals.*

My newfound corporate career served as another unexpected classroom. From a file clerk fumbling with dusty folders, I promoted into several roles and landed as an assistant operations manager running the operations of the courthouse. I relished the responsibility, the weight of each document which were stories unfolding within those walls. It was here, amidst the legal jargon and courtroom dramas, that I tasted the first bitter tang of leadership, navigating the treacherous waters of office politics and learning the delicate art of managing egos.

My role with the court glittered with even more purpose. The smooth running of the judicial system, the coordination of countless moving parts, held the weight of individual lives, of justice served. This, I realized with a jolt of pride, was my legacy, my contribution to the world, etched not in stone, but in the daily rhythm of a fair and just system. But within the confines of responsibility, another dream blossomed. A vision of a name in bold letters etched not on the court building, but on my own. It was a quiet symphony playing in the back of my mind, a melody fueled by the lessons learned, the challenges conquered, the potential glimpsed in the eyes of others. I could feel something different coming my way.

Before that something came, a roadblock would soon come, which was the sting of disrespect, however, lingered. Women who mirrored my own reflection, entrusted with the power to guide, turned into obstacles—I thought. The disillusionment was sharp, but it sparked a different kind of fire within me. If they, with their perceived advantages, could treat me with such disregard, it meant the path ahead, uncharted as it was, held the potential for something greater. There is a need for us to go through challenges to make us strong and ready for what's to come.

Toastmasters International was an organization I joined during my career with the Federal Judiciary. It was one of the best decisions I could have ever made. Toastmasters became my sanctuary, a platform where I shed my shyness and embraced the power of my voice. It was here, under the watchful eyes of mentors like Joan, Linda, and Terry, that I discovered the magic of storytelling, the ability to order words that resonated with the soul. Each hesitant speech, each stammering anecdote, chipped away at the fear, leaving in its wake a **budding** confidence.

After a few years of working with the agency, I felt it was time to pursue another goal I had in mind. Leaving my mother's house, a step both terrifying and liberating, wasn't an act of defiance, but an experiment in self-discovery. Building my first home wasn't just about creating a physical haven. It was another exercise in self-reliance, a testament to the resilience I carried from the projects. The experience, a collection of blueprints, permits, and contractor negotiations, birthed a new confidence, a hunger to build not just homes, but empires.

The miles that had separated my mother and I were bridged by the job application I'd given her, a tangible symbol of my desire to see her more since we were miles apart—her in Illinois and me in Indiana. Both of us had become dedicated servants of our communities, holding careers with two separate and distinct federal agencies.

After roughly two decades of service within the Federal Judiciary and establishing a family, the onset of COVID-19 served as an awakening for me. That thing that I had been feeling was nearing. Facing uncertainty about life and the world's future, I felt compelled to write a book dedicated to my daughters. I wanted to impart to them the legacy, love, and traditions I had instilled within our family, empowering them to carry on these values. Acknowledging my imperfections, I strived to do my best, just as I am doing now for all of you. With a need for someone to publish my very first book, I awoke one morning with the inspiration to start a publishing company. Taking immediate action, I sat at the computer, initiated the business, and phoned my mother, informing her of my impulsive decision. I declared that it would entail on-the-job training, with no room for refusal. From that moment, our journey began—a company with over 50 authors and counting, organizing events, making a positive impact in the community. Everything I learned from previous roles and interactions prepared me for this meaningful moment. I am a publisher, but it all starts with being attuned to the voices guiding us to move forward or to remain where we are because it is not always time to move. We must listen to the whispers of our heart and the echoes of our childhood dreams. Don't be afraid of the unknown, of the paths less traveled. The greatest discoveries often lie beyond the charted map, in the uncharted territories of self-exploration. Trust your instincts, embrace the stumbles, and celebrate the victories, big and small.

For you, like me, hold the power to write your own story. The inkwell is your spirit, the pen your determination, and the blank page a world of possibilities waiting to be explored. So, pick up your pen, speak your dreams into existence, and watch as they bloom, vibrant and magnificent, in the garden of your life. This is how a publisher is born, not from paper and ink, but from the courage to explore, the passion to create, and the belief in the power of your own voice.

This journey, however, isn't just mine to tell. Each chapter holds a space for your stories, your struggles, your triumphs, woven together to create resilience and inspiration. So, let your voice ring out, let your experiences paint the canvas, and together, we'll turn these scattered threads into a symphony of self-discovery, a testament to the unstoppable force of the human spirit.

I will repeat, this is the story of a publisher, but it can also be yours. So, turn the page and let the journey begin. For within you lies an author waiting to be unleashed, a voice yearning to be heard, and a story demanding to be told.

# CHAPTER 3:

## PROJECT NAVIGATION:

*The Parts of Your Story that will Release the Author from Within*

*"To be yourself in a world that is constantly trying to make you something else is the greatest accomplishment."* —Ralph Waldo Emerson

Life, like a well-crafted story, unfolds in chapters - some bursting with vibrant hues of joy, others etched in the sober tones of hardship. Each twist and turn, each whispered triumph and resounding trial, weaves the rich array of our being. But unlike a bound book on a dusty shelf, our stories remain dynamic, perpetually in flux, with every experience adding to the ever-evolving masterpiece. It wouldn't be appropriate to skip over the parts of the book that will unleash the author from within. Therefore, in this chapter, you will be introduced to those components of a real book, one that may be sitting on the very shelves of your home. This chapter serves as your classroom—an educational resource for those embarking on the journey of writing their own story. It outlines the key components of a book.

# THE FRONTMATTER

*Title page, copyright, dedication, acknowledgments, foreword, table of content and preface.*

Just as every journey begins with a map, every story finds its anchor in the *front matter*. The *title page*, a bold declaration of its essence, whispers promises of worlds yet to be explored.

The *copyright page*, a guardian of intellectual property, reminds us that even the most fantastical worlds rest on a foundation of reality and respect. Just as the *copyright* permissions and discussion questions ensure the longevity and engagement with the story, so too do we strive to leave a legacy, to ignite minds and inspire new journeys. The appendix or addendum, like tucked-away memories, provides additional context or insights, enriching the tapestry of our lives. The chronology, a map of time, reminds us of the flow of our experiences, showcasing how trials and triumphs have shaped the person we've become.

Then comes the *dedication and acknowledgments*, a tender inscription pouring gratitude onto the very pages that will hold our souls. This is where we acknowledge the guiding stars who illuminate our darkest nights, the hands that steady our trembling steps, the sound of ancestors whispering courage in our ears. No "you" stands alone, for every triumph bears the fingerprints of those who paved the way for us.

A *foreword* in a book serves as an introduction, often written by someone other than the author, providing context and background for the reader. It relates to our everyday lives in that it highlights the importance of perspective and the contributions of others in shaping our journeys. Just as a foreword sets the stage for the book, the guidance, support, and insights we receive from those around us help frame our experiences and influence our future paths. This interplay underscores how our lives are enriched by the shared wisdom and encouragement of mentors, friends, and family.

Before plunging into the heart of the story, a *table of contents* offers a glimpse of the chapters yet to unfold. It's a roadmap, a promise of adventures to come, whetting the reader's appetite for the trials and triumphs waiting within. Just as we scan this index of our lives, recognizing familiar landmarks and anticipating uncharted territories, so too does the reader navigate the words, seeking resonance and discovery.

The *preface*, a hushed preamble, sets the stage, offering a glimpse into the author's heart and mind. It's a whispered invitation, a bridge between the familiar and the unknown, where doubts are acknowledged, and vulnerabilities exposed. Here, the writer bares their soul, laying bare the motivations and insecurities that breathe life into their stories.

# THE BODY

*Introduction, Chapters, Main Story, Sections/Parts*

The *introduction*, a bold declaration of intent, throws open the doors to the narrative universe. It's the first step into the unknown, a hook that snags the reader's attention and propels them forward. Within these pages, the writer's voice finds its full resonance, setting the tone and rhythm for the chapters to come.

And finally, the story truly begins. *Chapters/Main-Story /Sections/Parts* in a book serve as the main divisions of the story, each containing a segment of the narrative. They provide structure, organization, and help guide the reader through the plot's progression. In life, chapters represent distinct phases or periods, each with its own set of experiences, challenges, and growth opportunities. Just like chapters in a book, these phases help shape our story, providing a sense of direction and marking important milestones along the way.

# THE BACKMATTER

*Epilogue, afterword/final thoughts, acknowledgments, postscript/final-thoughts, also by, about the author, glossary/references*

The *back matter*, like the closing paragraphs of a well-lived life, offers reflection and closure. The accolades, if present, are like trophies on a shelf, signifying the external validation of our struggles and victories. But true fulfillment lies not in accolades, but in the quietness of the "About the author" section, where the writer bares their soul once more, offering a glimpse into the beating heart behind the words.

An *epilogue* is a section that comes at the end of the main story, providing closure or additional insights into the characters' lives after the conclusion. Similarly, in life, the epilogue could symbolize reflection on past experiences, lessons learned, and how they continue to impact us as we move forward. It's a reminder that our stories don't end with one chapter but continue to evolve, offering opportunities for growth and reflection.

The conclusion of a book wraps up the main storyline, resolves conflicts, and ties up loose ends. It provides a sense of resolution and closure to the narrative. In our lives, conclusions represent moments of closure, acceptance, and understanding. They signify the end of one chapter and the beginning of another, allowing us to move forward with clarity and purpose.

An *afterword* is a section added by the author or someone closely connected to the book, offering additional commentary, insights, or context. It provides a deeper understanding of the story and its significance. Similarly, in life, the afterword could symbolize the wisdom and perspective gained from our experiences. It's a chance to share personal insights, lessons learned, and the impact they've had on our journey.

A *postscript/final thought(s)* is a brief note added at the end of a letter or document, often containing a final thought or message. In a book, it may offer a closing remark or reflection from the author. In life, the postscript represents those unexpected moments, final thoughts, or messages we encounter as we reflect on our journey. It's a reminder to cherish every moment, embrace serendipity, and find beauty in the unexpected twists and turns of life.

Both the "*Also By*" and "*About the Author*" sections serve to deepen the relationship between the reader and the author, much like how real-life interactions and personal histories build connections and understanding among people. The "*Also By*" section lists other works written by the same author. It can appear in the front or back matter of a book and provides readers with additional reading options from the same writer. Just as a professional might showcase their previous projects or work experiences on a resume or LinkedIn profile, the "Also By" section highlights an author's past achievements, helping to establish their credibility and body of work. While the "*About the Author*" section provides a brief biography of the author, it often includes personal background, career highlights, achievements, and sometimes personal anecdotes or philosophies. Similar to how introductions in real life help people get to know each other, the "About the Author" section gives readers a glimpse into who the author is, creating a personal connection. People share their stories to connect and relate to others. The "About the Author" section does the same by presenting the author's narrative, making their work more relatable and humanized.

The *glossary* of our lives remains ever evolving, each experience adding a new term, a fresh perspective. The index points us back to moments of significance. The *bibliography*, a testament to the influences that shaped our stories, acknowledges the voices that resonated within us, weaving their wisdom into the fabric of our own journeys. And finally, the bonus material, like hidden treasures discovered long after the initial exploration, offers unexpected gems: a secret anecdote, a forgotten photograph, a glimpse into alternate paths not taken.

Like a captivating *epigraph*, our lives echo with the voices of those who came before us. In their words, we find solace, understanding, and fuel for our own journeys. Whether it's a verse from Maya Angelou or a proverb read by your grandmother, these guiding quotes become signposts along the path, leading the way even when the way ahead seems masked in mist.

So as you navigate the chapters of your own life, know that just as these components are essential for crafting a compelling and impactful story in a book, they also play a vital role in shaping our own life narratives. Each phase, reflection, and moment of closure contributes to the richness and depth of our personal stories, making them truly fulfilling and impactful.  Remember - no story is complete without its trials and triumphs, its frontmatter, its backmatter, its chapters, and all the components of a true story.

Embrace the twists and turns, the laughter and tears, for each brushstroke adds depth and character to your masterpiece. Acknowledge the guiding stars who light your path, the scars that whisper lessons learned, and the echoes of wisdom that resonate within. Above all, craft your story with passion, vulnerability, and belief in the power of your own voice. For within each of us lies a story waiting to be told, experiences yearning to be shared, and a legacy yet to be written.

As you continue to turn the pages of this story, I urge you to think about sharing your trials and triumphs, your wisdom, and echoes of hope. Together, let our stories intertwine, creating a vibrant symphony of resilience. Let us navigate the landscape of our lives, appreciating every chapter, every scar, every victory. For in the journey of our stories, we find not only our own reflection, but a chorus of voices echoing through time, whispering a collective promise - that every life, no matter how ordinary, holds the potential for an extraordinary narrative.

Now, turn the page. Your story awaits.

# CHAPTER 4:
## Ink and Aspirations
### *Where Love Writes the First Draft*

*"The best love story is when you fall in love with the most unexpected person at the most unexpected time."*
—Unknown

They say everyone has a love story, an account that encompasses laughter, tears, and the tender dance of two souls intertwined. My love story, became the catalyst for a literary journey that transcended the confines of my heart, and blossomed into a platform for untold stories.

My publishing journey began, as love stories do, with a spark. It was the quiet communion of pen meeting paper that birthed my first book. Each sentence felt like a declaration of love, pouring out of my soul onto the crisp, blank, white pages. Can you relate?

But true love, they say, isn't a solo act. It thrives on connection, on the power of sharing and nurturing. And so, inspired by my own literary baptism, I set my sights on a new horizon: helping others embark on their own journeys of self-expression. It began with a single aspiring author. I saw in their words the same fire that had once burned within me, and with gentle guidance and nurturing, I helped them fan those flames into a radiant blaze. The moment their book, birthed from our collaboration, found its place available to bookstores, a masterpiece written into existence, was a turning point. It wasn't just their success I celebrated, but the realization that my love for storytelling and publishing could become a bridge for the masses to share their unique stories too.

# MY LOVE OF WRITING REVEALED

"Keep Him Coming Home with Love" originated from my hopes of building a deeper connection with my daughters, gained momentum due to the threat of the COVID-19 Pandemic. Uncertain of how long I would live because several people were dying from this viral infection, I wanted my daughters to know the story of how their dad and I met. I would encompass both the good and bad times. Our effort to infuse family values, traditions, and legacy into our lives became a central theme.

This four-book series serves as a representation of the four seasons in life. Book One, "*Be Intentional About Strengthening Your Bond*," symbolizes my summer, exploring the freshness of my relationships and concluding with rocky moments. Book Two, "*The Warmth of Your Home Determines the Temperature of Your Relationship,*" reflects my winter, a period of the continuous struggle within my relationship, but it focused on rediscovering myself after losing my identity while striving to be a good wife and mother that I only knew how to be. Book Three, "*Living Out Various Experiences through Conversation,*" corresponds to my fall. In this season, I interviewed the significant men in my life to assess the impact of both heroes and villains on the man I chose as my husband. And book four, yet unwritten, revolves around "*The Family that Prays Together Stays Together.*" By this point, I recognized that love alone isn't sufficient in a relationship. While it may sound melancholic, this realization marked my spring—a season of growth and renewal in understanding the complexities of sustaining a lasting connection. By the time you read this story of the making of a publisher, perhaps *Keep Him Coming Home with Love (KHCHwL),* book four, has found its words, with the hopes of finally having a relationship grounded in shared faith and resilience.

The book series *KHCHwL* is a testament of the true power of love in my life. Love doesn't just bloom within the confines of our hearts; it spills outward, staining the canvas of our lives with vibrant colors of passion, purpose, and the four seasons that we will all endure. This four-part series of words, interwoven with threads of, hope, and resilience, wasn't just a series of books; it was an invitation, a promise to those yearning to share their stories, to find understanding and recognizing the experiences shared from my eyes.

Nature's Alure, a fictional version of *Keep Him Coming Home with love* will add a fantasy yet marvel spin to my real-life. It will show the power of "Nature," who is me and how I allured my significant other into being in a relationship with me. But it also shows how the alluring backfired because he actually made me fall deeply in love with him as well.

# A PREVIEW OF NATURE'S ALLURE: THE PUPPET MASTER'S DANCE

You will embark on a captivating journey in the fiction novella, *"Nature's Allure: The Puppet Master's Dance,"* where Nature, a woman born from the earth's essence, discovers her alluring powers drawn from her own beauty. As she encounters Alex, a mysterious man immune to her charms, a web of deception unfolds, revealing him as the puppet master orchestrating her destiny. Nature grapples with limited healing abilities, questioning the purpose behind her existence. In a shocking twist, she must confront whether she can break free from Alex's control or remain a pawn in a mysterious game. Will Nature's untamed spirit guide her to forge her own destiny, or is she fated to dance to the puppet master's tune? "Nature's Allure" explores the delicate balance of power, seduction, and the spirit of nature that shape our destinies.

# IN CONCLUSION

So, as you turn the pages of this very book, remember that within you lies a story waiting to be told. A love story, perhaps, not in the traditional sense, but a love for your own voice, for your unique journey, for the power of your words to create and connect. Take inspiration from the ink that stains these pages, from the stories that rise from its depths. Embrace your own aspirations, nurture your fire, and let your story find its way into the world, its ready to breathe on its own.

Every voice and every experience deserves to be heard. And when we share our stories, when we weave them together with threads of love, we create a tapestry far more beautiful, far more impactful, than any one voice could ever achieve alone.

If you'd like to explore the themes of love, loss, resilience, and hope, pick up your copies of *"Keep Him Coming Home with Love."* Read between the lines as I share the genesis of navigating the challenges I faced, and the lessons learned along the way. You'll meet the people in my life who inspired my imagination onto these pages. But you must remember that the journey that you will embark on isn't just about my series. It's about birthing the series of your story. Know that your story matters and will touch others differently and like no other.

The world needs your voice, your unique perspective, and the shared experiences that only you can share. For within each of us lies a story waiting to be told.

Have you decided to share your story yet? If so, this is just the beginning.

# Chapter 5

## Chapters of Ambition

### *The Journey Takes Shape*

*"The journey of a thousand miles begins with one step."* --Lao Tzu

In my journey of becoming a publisher, it began with my story first, but if it were not for the authors who allowed me to collaborate with them, I could not hold the official name of publisher. The year was 2020, my best friend and a women named Tiffany Jackson had a dream to share their story and decided to take a leap of faith together with S.H.E. PUBLISHING LLC. I'd gone to high school with Sharaka, but Tiffany and I met through a mutual acquaintance.

I fondly recall a phone conversation with my friend Sharaka. It had been a while since we last spoke, so we took the opportunity to catch up. Remarkably, despite the gap in communication, our connection remained strong as if no time had passed. There was no guilt-tripping for not staying in touch; instead, we simply regrouped, exchanged updates, and made plans to spend more time together. Our mutual aim is clear: to nurture a robust and dependable relationship. As an only child, I've grown accustomed to solitude, yet I recognize the value of trust and friendship-building.

As Sharaka and my conversation unfolded, I confided in her about a book I had quietly written, without any prior announcement or promotion. It was a project dedicated solely to my daughters—the Keep Him Coming Home with Love series. In turn, she shared her own project, a story she'd title "Boss Rules." Initially intrigued by her concept, our discussion took an unexpected turn when she expressed her desire for me to publish her book. While publishing my own work was one thing, taking on someone else's was an entirely different venture. It would entail drafting agreements, crafting publishing packages, determining cost, and establishing a dedicated website for books. Despite my apprehension, Sharaka's encouragement bolstered my confidence. She assured me that if I could handle my own publication, hers would be a piece of cake. Though I lacked extensive experience, I took the leap, and before long, we successfully published her book, marking my official entry into the realm of publishing for others.

I am a true believer of the concept "word of mouth" and it proved true with the inception and experiences I've had running the operations of SHE PUBLISHING LLC. I recall another phone conversation with two of my other friends, a power hour session where we shared updates on our endeavors. As you can see, I like having these kinds of pow-wows. From that dialogue emerged the idea for another book launch, born from our desire to support each other's ventures, which is another story. Our conversation on the phone this particular evening was a simple exchange of ideas and support.

I'd say it was a couple of weeks later and one of those friends I was on the phone with was going about her day at work and unexpectedly a woman, Tiffany Jackson, approached her seeking a publisher for her book. Vita couldn't fathom why Tiffany had chosen her for such a revelation. Vita remembered the previous night speaking with me on the phone, a young black woman who had recently launched a publishing company. These connections never cease to amaze me. There was no apparent reason for Tiffany to approach Vita about her publishing needs, yet she did. Vita shared our information, and just like that, the deal was sealed. Fast-forward to the present, we'd successfully published a book by our second author, titled "*Making My Spirit Smile.*"

I, fueled by an ambition that had always simmered beneath the surface, saw in Sharaka and Tiffany's eyes a reflection of my own yearning. We were women who, like characters in our own stories, had climbed our respective mountains, each rung on the ladder of hard work, a testament to relentless perseverance. To stand tall amidst the imposing architecture of our stories was a victory, a "make-it" moment etched in every sleepless night and conquered challenge.

The pandemic, a storm cloud casting its shadow over the world, became the unexpected catalyst. It was in the quiet of those locked-down days that I dared to peek into the corners of my soul, unearthing stories, raw and vulnerable, begging to be shared. Sharing, but not revealing, a delicate dance between exposure and self-preservation.

Within the first year of having the publishing company, and the word-of-mouth referrals, I'd heard the words "your name proceeds you." It was a blessing that before we stepped into a room or venue, people had heard of SHE PUBLISHING LLC. At this point, I realized I wanted to host an annual conference. I didn't want to just be a platform for published authors, but I wanted this experience to be a haven for aspiring authors, a table crafted with the understanding that every writer needs their own place to sit, their own canvas to paint upon, and a form of appreciation I had for them believing in SHE PUBLISHING LLC. We weren't just building our own success, we were laying the groundwork for others, project by project, creating a world where ambition met opportunity, and dreams found a safe place to take root.

I vividly recall the trials and triumphs of orchestrating my inaugural conference. When I think back to that day, I can't believe the first conference only lasted three hours, and we only had a couple of platters of fruit and appetizers rather than a lavish meal. It was only expected for attendees to arrive in casual attire. However, the event's compelling content left attendees eager for more, leading to the expansion of the second conference, which became a two-day affair, and conference three, which was a three-day extravaganza.

Expecting similar challenges and moments of elation in planning Conferences Two and Three, I was met with new obstacles. Initially, filling seats posed a considerable challenge in the inaugural year. Convincing individuals to forego the comforts of home, especially following COVID-19, demanded an all-hands-on-deck approach. These annual conferences hold personal significance.

Specifically, the anticipation for the second conference, coupled with it being our first gala, heightened excitement. At this particular conference, we combined teaching spaces that allowed for more cohesive experiences, that came to be a great addition. Year Three brought on a new set of hurdles. We sold out!!! Though attendance was no longer a concern, securing reservations in advance proved tricky. Reflecting on these experiences, I resolved to dedicate even more time to planning and marketing with my team for the next conference.

The joy of marketing authors remained a highlight for conference three. From sharing snippets of their stories to providing training, we celebrated their contributions with a well-deserved dinner and entertainment, including a DJ and band battle, and a keynote speech by an Emmy-nominated film producer. I've always dared to dream big. I speak what I seek until I see what I've said. Our conference is where award-winning authors have been born.

I hope from this chapter you have found a resonance, a whisper of your own ambition stirring within. Remember, every journey begins with a single step, every chapter with a hesitant pen stroke. Don't wait for grand pronouncements or unforeseen encounters. The magic unfolds for those who choose to create.

So, dear reader, pick up your pen, your brush, and your voice and paint your own dreams onto the canvas of life. Don't be afraid to stumble, to doubt, to rewrite. For within the imperfections lies the truest beauty, the raw authenticity that resonates within you.

# CHAPTER 6:

## Building Success through Connections:

### *Master Your Lane and Create Your Blueprint*

*"We have the ability to write the blueprint for our own goals and decide how we want to pursue them. If we allow others to do it for us, we won't achieve our full potential to be the best we can be."*
— **Ellen J. Barrier**

The dream of being the *greatest of all time*, the undisputed champion in our chosen field can be attainable per my interpretation of Ellen J. Barrier's quote. Whether it's poetry, printing, pest control, or publishing, reaching the pinnacle of success seems like a distant peak, only achievable by a select few. But what if I told you that true mastery lies not in replicating someone else's path, but in carving your own unique lane and building a blueprint for sustainable success? This isn't about dethroning anyone; it's about recognizing that your journey, your experiences, and your connections are the tools you need to forge your own path to greatness.

My encounter with the world of publishing has taught me one undeniable truth: trying new things broadens your horizon and leads you to where you were meant to be. It's not about blindly chasing trends or imitating others; it's about exploring, stepping outside your comfort zone, and embracing the lessons that each experience offers. In this chapter, I want to share some of the invaluable insights I've learned from the diverse individuals who've graced my life, each playing a role in shaping the woman and the corporate-preneur I am today.

The principles of mentorship and collaboration shaped my journey through the guidance and wisdom of individuals from various walks of life. From Toastmasters to my bosses within the Federal Judiciary, from elementary school educators like Mr. Niznik and Ms. Diane Shulla to the multitude of authors under the SHE PUBLISHING LLC umbrella, I've both received and bestowed invaluable support and advice.

Samuel I Jackson, author of "Wounds Can Heal Even if Scars Remain," instilled in me the significance of implementing a SYSTEM (Saving Your Self Time, Energy, and Money) to streamline operations and delegate tasks effectively, thus aiding in the promotion of SHE PUBLISHING LLC.

Bertina Power, author of "The Power of You! No One is You, and that is your POWER!," underscores the importance of note-taking as a cornerstone of success—a lesson I've found to be profoundly true.

Pastor Henry L. Razor's teachings emphasize the notion that one is the best advocate for their own narrative, a principle he exemplifies admirably.

Shartia "Love" Jones and Dr. Calenthia Miller have imparted the vital lesson of self-love amidst the whirlwind of endeavors.

There's more!!! I count myself fortunate to have been surrounded by such a wealth of mentors throughout my life, serving as emotional reservoirs that continually replenish and maintain a positive balance in my emotional bank account.

One of the most potent connections in the publishing industry was forged through my mother. It's because of her and one of my daughters that I met Jon Ross, the Emmy-nominated film producer. It's a reminder that often, the opportunities we seize wouldn't exist without the connections woven by the people around us. We underestimate the ripple effect of our interactions, the way a seemingly casual encounter can trigger a chain reaction of possibilities. Remember, you may be the one closing the deal, but acknowledge the steppingstones, the moments of grace, and the individuals who nudged you onto the path.

But connections are not just about chance encounters; they're also about fostering relationships, nurturing partnerships, and learning to navigate difficult dynamics. Each experience in our lives will offer invaluable lessons on building a positive and supportive network. Learn to identify the "Know-It-Alls" who drain your energy and surround yourself with people who bring peace and positivity to your life. It's not about cutting people off; it's about creating a circle of trust and collaboration that empowers you to thrive.

Remember, "show, and don't always tell." Actions speak louder than words, and demonstrating your worth through consistent effort is far more impactful than self-promotion. Speak your dreams into existence, visualize your goals, and then get to work making them a reality. Don't get stuck in the planning phase; embrace the spirit of "try it and see" and learn from your failures. Write down your plans, work your plan with unwavering dedication, and celebrate every single solitary milestone along the way.

The feeling of belonging is essential, so create your own circle, your own table, your own entourage. Make noise, share your dreams, and connect with like-minded individuals who inspire and elevate you. Your network is your safety net, your sounding board, and your source of endless possibilities. Remember, people remember how you make them feel; so, prioritize kindness, respect, and genuine connection in every interaction.

Building local connections is paramount. Your target audience isn't just a faceless demographic; they're real people in your community. Engage with them, understand their needs, and tailor your offerings to their interests. Be present, be accessible, and show them the value you can bring to their lives.

Also, learning to choose your battles is a crucial skill. Some battles deserve your determination, while others are simply not worth the emotional drain. Reflect on your values, assess the situation, and prioritize your energy expenditure. Remember, not every fight needs to be fought, and sometimes, walking away is the most powerful victory.

The next chapter will dig into how I leveraged existing resources, effectively utilizing the skills of friends and family while avoiding unnecessary financial obligations. These stories will exemplify the advantages of resourcefulness and the supportive power of a community. Building a successful business doesn't always require external resources. My journey, in many ways, was fueled by the invaluable knowledge and skills generously shared by those around me. From website building to graphic design, I tapped into the talents of friends and family, forming a support network that enabled me to grow without breaking the bank. Remember, true wealth lies not just in financial abundance, but in the richness of your connections and the willingness to learn from one another. This isn't about relying solely on others; it's about recognizing the strengths within your own community and leveraging them to create a shared win. You become a part of a vibrant system, where skills flow freely, and mutual support paves the way for collective success. It's like planting a seed that blossoms into a bountiful garden, each individual flourishing alongside the others.

This journey for me also hasn't been solely about achieving personal goals; it has been about inspiring others and leaving a legacy of empowerment. My dream is to build a platform, a haven for aspiring authors to find their voice, hone their craft, and navigate the often-daunting world of publishing.

With that said, I ask you to imagine a world where connections don't just lead to personal victories but ignite a ripple effect of literary excellence. Authors not just competing, but collaborating, lifting each other up, and enriching the literary landscape through the blends of their unique stories. This is the world I dream of, and it all starts with taking that first step, with connecting, with sharing, and with believing in the transformative power of storytelling.

The world is your stage, your community your support system, and your voice—your most potent instrument. Use it to forge your own path, build your own table, and leave an indelible mark on the world, one story, one connection, one dream at a time.

Remember, you are not alone on this journey. We are all interconnected. So, reach out, share your voice, and let our collective stories and dreams resonate through the ages. Together, we can rewrite the narrative, not just of our own lives, but of the world around us. Let the ink flow, let the connections bloom, and let our stories take flight.

Are you ready?

# CHAPTER 7:

## PEAK POTENTIAL

*Unleashing Your Daily Brilliance*

*"Most brilliance arises from ordinary people working together in extraordinary ways."* – Roger Von Oech

When I contemplate tapping into my daily brilliance, a gift inherent in all of us, I am drawn to reflections on history and *"My Daily Bread,"* a cherished prayer book my grandmother Mable faithfully read each day.

Growing up, I didn't always grasp the significance of history; as a child, it often felt distant and incomprehensible. However, with maturity, I've come to appreciate its importance. Reflecting on the sacrifices and struggles of our ancestors, who paved the way for the freedoms I enjoy today, brings a bittersweet feeling. They exemplified true strength. Conversations with my children about the history of slavery evoke mixed emotions. Yet, hearing my 9-year-old daughter express gratitude for our present freedoms and acknowledge the role of figures like Abraham Lincoln fills me with humbleness. Witnessing her humility and appreciation underscores the importance of acknowledging our shared past, as well as the progress we've made.

From my personal experiences and those yet to unfold, it's clear that unleashing our daily brilliance is a collective endeavor. It's about recognizing the angels—be they family, teachers, friends, or mentors—who have guided us along the way. For me, it's been my significant other, my fathers, my daughters, teachers, friends, bosses, authors, among others. Yet, I recognize that my journey is rooted in the generational prayers of my mother, grandmothers Mabel and Janice, and even my great-grandmothers whom I've never met. Their prayers have provided a steadfast foundation through life's myriad challenges, **and no one person or fleet can break the bounds of those prayers.**

In addition to daily prayers, I rely on guiding principles that propel me forward in my journey as a publisher, mother, daughter, and all of the other roles that I hold. I share these principles with the hope that they may inspire or resonate with you.

# BE OKAY WITH BEING IN YOUR LANE AND PLAYING THE CARDS OF LIFE THAT YOU'RE DEALT Otherwise, You May Be Grasping for Something You Can't Handle

*"Some people lead their life while others accept their life."*
*—Gallup*

I recall the day my doorbell rang, and upon opening the door, I was greeted by a UPS delivery person. For them, it brought a genuine sense of joy to have delivered a package to my doorstep. *"Are you the owner of SHE PUBLISHING LLC?" he inquired with a warm smile. "I've been delivering several packages to you. My name is Mike. Nice to meet you."* At that moment, I felt a glimmer of celebrity status. Yet, amidst the excitement of SHE PUBLISHING LLC gaining recognition, I couldn't ignore the realization that with fame comes both benefits and challenges—would my past experiences, including growing up in the Robert Taylor projects, prepare me for what lay ahead?

Little did I know that my upbringing in the Robert Taylor projects in Chicago, Illinois would later serve as the backdrop for an intriguing journey and book titled—*from PROJECTS to PUBLISHER*. The title alone sparks curiosity, but it's the subtitle, 'Navigating the Chapters of Life While Maximizing Your OWN Lane,' is what speaks volumes. Not everyone is destined for the spotlight or celebrity status. Personally, I prefer wealth and influence behind the scenes, away from the public scrutiny that accompanies fame. The *allure* of celebrity often masks the unseen struggles and challenges that come with it.

I once came across a thought-provoking image on social media depicting the disparity between public perception and the harsh reality of success. Behind the glitz and glamor lie stories of stalking, addiction, exploitation, and financial ruin. However, it's essential to acknowledge that many individuals in the industry excel and use setbacks as steppingstones to greatness.

As the CEO of SHE PUBLISHING LLC, I've experienced vulnerabilities firsthand. Yet, with a solid support system and a carefully curated inner circle, I've navigated these challenges with resilience. With that said, I am only human, which makes me imperfect. My true team comprises of those who believed in me from the start, offering their expertise without expecting anything in return. They unknowingly laid the foundation for an empire that extends beyond me, encompassing the well-being of their families too.

*Unleash your daily brilliance.*

# IT'S OKAY TO BE INTENTIONAL, IT'S NOT OKAY TO BE FAKE

*"Write the Story You Want to Live."*
*–Shenitha Finesse Anniece*

Whether you're pursuing a career as an author or in a different profession, being intentional is crucial. As I share advice with our authors, I invite you to reflect on your current profession and consider ways to purposefully drive your success. One piece of advice I often give to both first-time and seasoned authors is to prioritize building relationships within their industry. While it's essential to research and develop skills, networking remains key.

Throughout this book, my message has been consistent: *build your own table*. This concept applies here as well, albeit in a slightly different context. I encourage authors to visit local bookstores, offering them resources to easily locate these establishments. Once they've compiled a list, I advise them to visit these stores, fostering connections and allowing booksellers to become acquainted with them personally. By being a positive presence in their stores, and a positive servant within their community, authors can establish rapport and potentially secure shelf space for their books at an affordable rate or for $free.99. Moreover, by promoting their own books, they inadvertently promote the bookstores, creating a mutually beneficial relationship.

Authors can take further intentional steps by organizing local book tours, both at bookstores and libraries in their area. It's not necessary to overextend oneself; even targeting a few key locations can yield significant results. However, it's important to ensure that these relationships are genuine; if a connection feel forced or insincere, it's best to let it go.

In addition, taking gradual steps towards these goals can be advantageous. By pacing oneself and focusing on quality over quantity, authors can effectively navigate the process of building relationships and promoting their work. This approach, characterized by intentionality and authenticity, ultimately leads to long-term success.

*Unleash your daily brilliance.*

# MAKE SMALL FOOTPRINTS TOWARDS YOUR BIG DREAMS

*"Go the extra mile. It's never crowded."*
—Unknown

I've made the bold decision to establish a bookstore to showcase the numerous books I've published, providing a dedicated space for our authors' works to shine. My vision extends beyond mere shelves of books; I dream of a place where our authors' faces adorn the walls, transforming them into the celebrated figures of our community. Imagining innovative features like book vending machines only fuels my excitement for this venture.

To turn this dream into reality, I've taken deliberate small steps forward. I reached out to the bank to understand their requirements and enlisted the help of professionals to craft a comprehensive business plan. Drawing on my innate strengths, I've sought out new information and ideas to inform our bookstore's development.

Moreover, I've assembled an exceptional team to assist in running this establishment, ensuring that we have the expertise and dedication necessary for success. With each passing day, I'm inching closer to realizing this ambitious goal. Whether it comes to fruition this year, the next, or in the future, I am steadfast in my determination to see this dream come to life like it did in the game of LIFE I played, knowing that every effort brings me one step closer to achievement.

*Unleash your daily brilliance.*

# LEAVE IT BETTER THAN YOU FOUND IT

*We owe it to each other, our children, our co-workers, our significant others, our neighbors, and our family, to leave it better than we found it.*

Having both a nine-to-five, and a five-to-nine, *or a six-to-twelve*—as my sister in publishing often says, is perfectly fine. I take pride in being what I call a corporate-preneur because it has allowed me the opportunity to *unleash my daily brilliance*. Two prominent things guided me in this pursuit. Firstly, a quote I encountered in a colleague's office: "*Speak what you speak until you see what you've said.*" Secondly, insights from a leadership round table facilitated by my strengths coach, Beverly Griffeth-Bryant, where we discussed the concept of "*Leave it Better Than You Found It.*"

During one of these meetings, a colleague presented the idea of "*Leave it Better Than You Found It,*" and it resonated deeply with me and all those who were in attendance. Imagine if we all made it our mission to leave every situation better than we found it – what a profound impact we could have on our communities, workplaces, families, and the environment. Many shared their practices, from simple acts like making the bed or sharing information with coworkers to more profound gestures of leadership. I was touched by one person's story of someone sharing that one of their co-workers had cleaned their oatmeal bowl, demonstrating how small acts can make a big difference.

In my role as a mother and significant other, whether it's tidying up the space before anyone else wakes up or ensuring a welcoming environment for my families return from a trip, I find joy in improving the space around me.

In my role as a publisher, and in my everyday interactions in my nine-to-five career, I've always strived to leave things better without even consciously realizing it. It's ingrained in me to create a positive impact wherever I go. The publishing industry may have a strong reputation, but I am driven to challenge the status quo and leave my mark by doing things uniquely and making them better than I found them. I aspire to be a trailblazer in this field, continuously *unleashing my daily brilliance* to elevate the industry and inspire others to refrain from being judgmental and to follow suit.

*Unleash your daily brilliance.*

# HAVING THE FAITH TO JUST DO IT | OVERTHINKING LEADS TO STAGNATION

*Draw strength from faith and the*
*power of prayer to navigate life's uncertainties.*
*—Unknown*

This newfound awareness of serving others as a publisher was liberating. I was finally crafting something special—paving my own path, guided by my unique strengths fueled by passion. But self-knowledge, while crucial, is just the first step. The next? Action. Audacious, consistent action. I can remember attending a fundraiser event and showcased my "Newsletter Mag"! When a stranger, with eyes sparkling with recognition, pointed out the untapped potential of the name, I didn't hesitate. I marched straight to GoDaddy, purchased the domain, and planted the first seed of what would become my passion project—The BNB Newsletter Mag.

Nike was right, "Just do it." Overthinking leads to stagnation, to dreams gathering dust in the attic of our minds. It's the act of doing, the imperfect and messy first step, that propels us forward. Don't wait for grand pronouncements or cosmic signs. Start small, take that one action, and let the momentum carry you.

*Unleash your daily brilliance.*

# ACT YOUR WAY UP

*You become what you believe. You are where you are today in*
*your life based on everything you have believed.*
*—Oprah Winfrey*

Before you hold a formal title, you already possess those qualities. This is a mantra I often repeat. I consider myself fortunate to have built an impressive career resume. Sometimes, I fail to fully grasp the extent of my achievements, but it's because I've consciously steered my career journey towards greatness. In every role I've held, I've infused a part of myself into it, and I believe this is essential for everyone to do. During this period of my life, mid-teen years to becoming a young adult, I didn't realize that others saw potential in me that I hadn't yet recognized in myself. As an adult, I now see this potential in my children and others. Sometimes, we try to instill in them the potential we see, but true realization of one's potential only comes when they recognize it within themselves and step into their purpose.

As mentioned in the start of this story, I recall an opportunity provided by my clerk of court, who entrusted me to organize a leadership retreat for my supervisors. It was a once-in-a-lifetime opportunity that many might overlook, failing to see its inherent purpose. This experience played a pivotal role in shaping my path as a publisher. It propelled me towards new experiences and brought me closer to discovering my purpose.

Throughout the project of organizing a leadership retreat, I encountered tasks I had never tackled before. So, what did I do? I embraced the concept of "acting my way up." I assumed the role, behaving as though I knew exactly what I was doing, instead of saying *this is above my pay grade*. On the other hand, it's important to note that seeking assistance when needed is vital. I drafted the necessary contracts to secure our instructor, delegated responsibilities, and assembled a team of individuals who possessed the skills I lacked, my supervisors. Each person played an important role in ensuring the success of the retreat. Although I'd already had the title of Assistant Operations Manager, in essence, I acted as a *Chief Executive of Operations* which could be a role in my possible future. I encourage you to adopt a similar approach—practice *"acting your way up"* as it brings you closer to achieving your goals.

*Unleash your daily brilliance.*

# CONTINUOUS LEARNING & NEVER STOP TRYING NEW THINGS

*Remain open to new experiences and*
*commit to lifelong learning or sharing.*

Step outside your comfort zone, explore uncharted territories, and discover what resonates with you. Whether it's a new cereal at the grocery store or a bold decision in your business, every experiment provides valuable insights and shapes your unique perspective. I tried a new thing. I wrote a book, and I started a publishing company. Publishing was never something I envisioned doing growing up as a kid. The professions that I knew of were doctors, lawyers, actresses, etc. There are several professions that I didn't know of until my adult life. Trying something new is what landed me to do what I have been passionate about. In a board game of LIFE, I became a brain surgeon, not saying that I would take it that far in my real-life, but hey, you never know. This section is supposed to encourage you to try new things and not let anyone talk you out of it. Try new things that will be of benefit to you and those around you. Serving others is a beautiful thing.

*Unleash your daily brilliance.*

# DON'T UNDERESTIMATE THE POWER OF YOUR EXISTING NETWORK

*"Show me your friends and I'll show you your future."* ....
*—Unknown*

One of the most empowering realizations during this journey of becoming a publisher was the strength found in collaboration. You are the star of your own narrative, yes, but the stage is rarely a solitary platform. Connect with other "stars," individuals who complement your strengths and fill the gaps in your own skill set. Surround yourself with doers, with action-oriented individuals who can propel you forward when your own engine sputters.

And don't underestimate the power of your existing network. Look around you, within your circle of friends and family. Chances are, you're surrounded by untapped potential, individuals with natural abilities waiting to be harnessed. Consider the Strengthsfinder assessment for yourself and your loved ones, discover those hidden talents, and co-create opportunities for mutual benefit.

Early on, I initiated an experience within my immediate family, inviting my daughters, who were old enough, to take the StrengthsFinder assessment. The CliftonStrengths™ Assessment, previously known as StrengthsFinder, is a personal development tool created by Gallup, a research and analytics firm. Rooted in positive psychology, it emphasizes the idea that individuals can attain significant success and satisfaction by leveraging their strengths instead of focusing on their weaknesses. It proved to be an eye-opening journey. Through this assessment, we gained insight into each other's leading personality traits, gaining clarity on our motivations and approaches. This shared understanding has since fueled both personal and professional endeavors within and beyond our family circle.

The inception of SHE PUBLISHING LLC was deeply influenced by this experience. I distinctly remember recognizing and harnessing the talents of those closest to me. As the developer, creator, and curator of SHE, I integrated elements of my own identity, with "S.H.E." representing the first three letters of my name. My mother assumed the role of maximizer and innovations manager within the company. Her ability to extract the full potential from ideas, often surpassing my own expectations, was invaluable. My sister-in-law's passion for literature and keen eye for detail made her an indispensable asset. She not only provided insightful feedback and editing expertise but also served as a sounding board for new concepts. Additionally, she offered invaluable guidance as an in-house therapist, alerting me to potential pitfalls and providing essential perspective.

My daughter J. Alexis and cousin Anita effortlessly cultivated a substantial following through their innate ability to engage and connect with others. Their contributions, along with those of our dedicated authors, have been instrumental in shaping our online presence and community outreach efforts. Another daughter, J. Camille, possesses remarkable photography skills and an innovative approach to business management, consistently exceeding expectations with her creative solutions.

The collective efforts of these individuals, alongside other dedicated contributors who generously donate their time, have been important in driving the growth of SHE PUBLISHING LLC. Their commitment and dedication embody the essence of our organization, transcending mere titles to embody the spirit of SHE long before it was officially recognized.

"Friends and family with benefits," I like to call them. Not the transactional kind, of course, but individuals who bring expertise, passion, and support to your endeavors, enriching your journey and propelling you closer to your dreams. Remember, you don't need to climb the mountain alone. Sometimes, all it takes is a helping hand, a shared vision, and the belief in each other's potential to reach the summit, together.

*Unleash your daily brilliance.*

# LET YOUR BRAIN REST FROM THE NOISE

*Taking time to do nothing often brings everything into perspective.*
*—D. Zantamata*

November 20, 2023, I recall leaving work, boarding the Metra train, and settling in for the 20-minute ride to my car, and syncing my headphones to my Galaxy Samsung. But as I walked down the stairs and stepped off the train, a sudden, searing pain shot from my knee to my ankle, altering my ability to walk. In that fleeting moment, my life changed. It serves as a stark reminder of how swiftly circumstances can shift, prompting me to avoid dwelling on ideas for too long, lest I miss crucial opportunities, like the chance to hear my grandmother's stories.

But let's return to the matter at hand – my mobility. Arriving home, I took a painkiller and rested, convinced it was merely a fluke. Awakening later, I found myself immobilized by excruciating pain. Fast forward to the doctor's orders for an MRI. I've never been fond of these machines; they're noisy and confining. Lying there, I struggled to quiet my mind. Unused to downtime, I found the experience unsettling. Perhaps it was a blend of anxiety and perpetual motion, a life always in motion.

Surviving the MRI ordeal, I resolved to integrate brain-resting practices into my daily routine. I had to learn, and I am still learning, how to disconnect from technology, to embrace moments of stillness without guilt. Accepting that some tasks may remain unfinished, I prioritize communication, recognizing my role as a business owner and leader. I've learned to appreciate leisurely walks, bike rides, and indulging in guilty pleasures, crucial steps in nurturing my peace of mind. I extend this advice to you, for it's a vital practice.

I also reflect on the loss of hearing in my left ear, a frightening experience. Though I'm grateful for divine healing and for retaining hearing in one ear, adapting to partial deafness has become a seamless challenge. It underscores the importance of mental rest and resilience in the face of adversity. So, I urge you to rest your mind from the noise, for while tomorrow isn't guaranteed, some tasks simply aren't meant to be completed.

*Unleash your daily brilliance.*

# DON'T RUSH PERFECTION; THINGS ARE DELAYED FOR A REASON

*There is a time to let things happen and
a time to make things happen.*

There have been numerous occasions when tasks remained unfinished, seemingly due to delays or setbacks. Yet, in hindsight, I realize these delays were often a form of protection. There are books left unpublished and individuals unsigned, all for significant reasons. If these processes had proceeded as initially planned, I would have undoubtedly encountered greater challenges and turmoil along the way. This concept brings to mind the events of 9/11. Consider those individuals who were delayed for work or missed their train, initially frustrated but ultimately spared from the tragedy that unfolded. Sometimes, delays or missed opportunities serve to safeguard us from unseen dangers.

Reflecting on personal experiences, I recall a planned trip to Caracas, Spain, with the intention of immersing myself in the culture for a month to learn Spanish. However, a medical concern arose, prompting my doctor to advise against the trip. While it may seem like a disappointment at the time, I now understand that it was a blessing in disguise. The cancellation of the trip allowed me to invest in building my first home—a tangible asset for my children's future. I intend to hold onto this home, ensuring my children have real estate assets to inherit or leverage.

The delays and detours in life often lead to extraordinary blessings. Embracing these delays as opportunities for growth and protection is essential. Perhaps a missed promotion shields you from a toxic work environment or boss, or a delayed book publication paves the way for the birth of a successful publishing venture. In essence, delays are not denials; they are simply redirections towards something better suited for our journey.

*Unleash your daily brilliance.*

# GRATITUDE AND ACTS OF KINDNESS FROM THE HEART

*Cultivate a mindset of gratitude for those who have supported and influenced you.*

I've found that giving away freebies has often resulted in a significant return, sometimes even triple, or quadruple the initial investment. It's important not to be solely focused on making sales and getting paid for every little thing. At SHE PUBLISHING LLC, for instance, we held an annual gala for our authors to attend, which resulted in a packed house for our third-year conference. The buzz generated from our free interviews with our authors on the ShePub network, complete with gift giveaways, has significantly increased our following. This not only spreads awareness of our publishing company but also increases the likelihood of someone recommending us to aspiring authors.

*Unleash your daily brilliance.*

# KNOW YOUR AUDIENCE, THE BLESSINGS IN DISGUISE

*"Look at your problems as problems & they'll continue to hold you down. See them as blessings in disguise & that's what they truly become." --Unknown*

Understanding one's audience and the blessings that come with it has become clear to me after being in this industry for only three years. Growth is a continual process, and sharing stories, whether officially published or not, contributes to one's legacy. Knowing who you're working with is crucial; don't jeopardize potential collaborations due to a lack of understanding. While many advocate for knowing one's worth, it's essential to realize that worth extends beyond monetary value; it encompasses the investments that lead to building an empire.

While many have expressed interest in partnering with SHE PUBLISHING LLC, discernment is key. Some proposals may seem like scams, while others are genuine opportunities. As a growing publishing company, we try to be cautious not to overextend ourselves financially. Researching the target audience is important; pricing strategies must appeal to both major players and smaller clients. It's unrealistic to expect payment that exceeds what one may earn in a month, but considering the potential for global expansion and long-term growth is crucial.

Sometimes, simply aligning with someone's dream and vision is payment enough. And for those who can't see the value beyond monetary gain, consider the exposure and credibility gained from associating with reputable figures or brands. When people believe in you and your dream, like we believed in Dr. Martin Luther King's dream, standing alongside someone with a shared vision yields more significant rewards than immediate financial gain, any day.

*Unleash your daily brilliance.*

# RESILIENCE IN THE MOMENTS OF CHALLENGE, *THAT LIFE WILL BRING*, KNOW THAT YOU ARE BECOMING

*Embrace challenges as opportunities for growth and persevere in the face of adversity.*

I proudly wear layers upon layers of challenges on my sleeve, like badges of honor. These challenges have strengthened me, making me more resilient with each passing day. In the midst of these trials, it's often difficult to see beyond the immediate struggle. Challenges can come from unexpected sources, even from those closest to us, like family, friends, or even acquaintances seeking solace in shared misery.

But despite the darkness that challenges may bring, there's always a glimmer of hope on the horizon amidst the forest of trees of the unseen sun. I recall a moment returning home from vacation, only to find water flooding from a broken pipe. In that initial panic, I found a strange comfort, a faith that everything would be alright. And indeed, with time, the situation turned around. The once-flooded home was renovated and ready to be rented out. I moved into a new home, one built on prayers and hopes, while simultaneously renewing my wedding vows in a ceremony inspired by my favorite TV series "*Game of Thrones.*"

Life's storms can leave us feeling overwhelmed, whether it's financial struggles, heartbreaking news, or health challenges. But in those moments, we must remind ourselves of our resilience as children of a higher power. Every challenge we face has the potential to either build us up or break us down. And if we're still standing, still breathing, even after the toughest moments, we know we have the strength to persevere.

As we navigate these challenges and chapters of life, let's not forget to pray positive prayers of hope for those that we know and are responsible for, following the example set by our ancestors and loved ones. Even in their darkest moments, they prayed for us without our knowledge, guiding us through life's trials. Now, it's our turn to carry on that tradition, offering silent prayers for those we hold dear.

Let's continue to practice what we preach, continuing to face challenges with faith, knowing that each hurdle brings us closer to the blessings that await on the other side.

*Unleash y**our** daily brilliance.*

# WASH YOUR HANDS

*"It's never too late or too early to work towards being the healthiest you."*
–Unknown

Last but certainly not least, make sure to wash your hands as often as you can. It will keep you well and in good health. It helps to prevent the spread of germs and illnesses. Just as thoroughly cleansing our hands can safeguard our physical well-being, so too can starting each day with a clean slate contribute to our overall mental and emotional health.

Each morning presents an opportunity for renewal (*clean hands*), a chance to leave behind the worries and mistakes of yesterday and approach the new day with a fresh and clean perspective. Similarly, ending each day on a positive note, reflecting on accomplishments, and expressing gratitude, serves as a form of closure. Embracing this daily ritual acknowledges the uncertainty of tomorrow while affirming our commitment to making the most of the present moment. Again, just as washing our hands protects our bodies from harm, embracing each day with a clean slate and ending it on a positive note can safeguard our mental and emotional well-being, ensuring that we approach life with resilience and optimism.

May these principles serve as guideposts on your journey toward unleashing your own daily brilliance. Embark on your own journey of self-discovery. Uncover your strengths, embrace your individuality, and take that first action, however small or imperfect. Remember, your daily brilliance is not a sudden spark; it's a fire waiting to be ignited. Gather your fellow "stars," leverage the talents of your network, and light up the world with the collective dazzle of your unleashed potential.

The stage is yours, the possibilities endless. What will you unleash today?

# CHAPTER 8:

## CONFESSIONS OF A PUBLISHER

*Desires, Decisions, Disappointments, and the Dress*

*"The size of your success is measured by the strength of your desire: the size of your dream; and how you handle disappointment along the way."*
–Robert Kiyosaki

*B*efore I begin with my taxi cab confessions of a publisher, I must say that I have one of the best careers in the world. I get to meet people like you and me who are ordinary people doing extraordinary things. And my *extraordinary* as a publisher is made up of the hidden layers of this profession – the desires that fuel our drive, the decisions that shape our paths, the disappointments that sometimes sting, and the ever-present question: who will inherit this legacy?

This chapter is about peeling back the layers of publishing and revealing what I've learned during this three (3) year tenure of my real-life in the game. I will hold up a mirror to the industry, reflecting not just the glamor of book launches and award ceremonies, but also what could be the quiet struggles, the hours and hours of hard work, and the communications with the authors who are passionate about their projects.

In this field, I've learned that passion can go both ways; it's a double-edge sword. Some people are driven by a passion to pursue their dreams, while others may be equally passionate about undermining those dreams. Often, people don't realize the impact of their actions. They may judge entire groups, places, or projects based on a single negative experience. It's important not to be narrow-minded. Keeping an open mind leads to open doors, new opportunities, and life-long relationships. Embracing a broader perspective allows for growth and the chance to achieve your dreams despite the challenges.

As I mentioned in an earlier chapter, one becomes a professional long before the formal title is bestowed upon them. The essence of leadership, for instance, is not confined to the moment one receives a title; a true leader embodies those qualities well before the official recognition. In my own experience, I came to realize that I had already embraced the role of a publisher, even before the formal title was assigned to me.

The aspiration to become a publisher was rooted in my passion for the love of literature, and learning from someone else's story, which is a commitment to sharing information. It was being able to do what I'd hoped to do with my grandmother, who I'd lived with in the projects. SHE PUBLISHING LLC would become the platform to share so that stories were not taken to the grave. This inner calling, unbeknownst to me at the time, had already shaped my actions and decisions, aligning me with the responsibilities and qualities associated with being a publisher.

But desires, like dreams, need a roadmap to become reality. My decision to create SHE Publishing LLC was an overnight decision. I don't sit in decision making too long. Not to mention, there were seeds planted years ago along the way that nurtured what has become my passion; my grandmother's belief; my husband starting his YouTube channel; and my own fierce determination. Now, this company stands as a testament to that decision, a potential vessel for my desires – not just financial success, but the freedom to be present for my family, to connect more with my children, and to finally be of support to them as I want to be, *as I thought*.

My grandmother Mabel's wise counsel echoes in my mind: "If you can't say anything nice, don't say anything at all." While navigating through this particular chapter, I find myself compelled to break this rule, but I won't because hearing her voice also reminds me to remember that we are all human, and extending grace is essential, just as I would wish to receive it.

Confessions of a Publisher is a platform that sheds light that building the foundation of a company requires constant reinvestment. Some may mistakenly assume that publishers reap substantial profits from book sales, but that's far from the truth. Me and our sister companies pour our hearts into every aspect of our work, from novices to seasoned authors alike. Running a publishing company entails expenses for yearly conferences, interviews, marketing efforts, custom packaging, featuring authors on BNB Newsletter Magazine covers, and managing author pages, among other investments. Our aim is to craft an immersive experience because, ultimately, life is about gathering stories to share.

The decision to launch "Confessions of a Publisher" wasn't driven by a desire to complain; it was a call for transparency, a counterpoint to the negativity that often surrounds this industry. I believe in empowerment, in giving aspiring authors the tools they need to navigate this complex world of publication. The lack of knowledge can lead to misunderstandings and disappointments.

The aftermath of the COVID-19 pandemic disrupted our ability to communicate directly with companies via phone, causing a decline in customer service standards as the world changed rapidly. Despite this, SHE PUBLISING LLC has made ourselves available through multiple channels, including email, website, social media, business phone, and personal lines—text messaging. We encourage our authors to utilize these various methods to ensure communication is maintained. Reflecting on my experiences, there are a few standout moments that have significantly contributed to my growth running the operations of a publishing company.

# DEVELOPMENT:
# THE AUTHORS' ORIENTATION

*"Knowledge becomes power only when*
*you put it to use."* –Unknown

My StrengthsFinder assessment (*a personal and professional development tool created by a research and analytics company call Gallup*) revealed that my top signature theme is "Developer," and this truly resonates with me. For as long as I can remember, I've always had a passion for developing others, and now I have a name for what I've been doing for all these years. I bring this talent into every role or career I take on. Throughout my journey from growing up in the projects to taking on real written projects to becoming a publisher, I've learned that empowering our authors through sharing information benefits us and them significantly in the long run.

Given the complexity of information in the publishing industry, some of which is often overlooked, one of our authors suggested we implement a continuous support program for authors. This program would be available throughout the year and could be updated as needed. Acting swiftly, we devised a program the very next day. We shared it with the requesting author, asked for their input on any additions or modifications, and with their feedback, we collaboratively created our pilot program: the Authors' Orientation.

To ensure the program's success, I involved our sister publishing companies, who contributed to and helped deliver the content. The inaugural Authors' Orientation spanned over a period of three days, with sessions held in the morning, evening, and weekends to accommodate varying schedules. This flexibility was crucial as some authors work during the day, while others work in the evening and/or weekends.

Unfortunately, authors who miss these orientations, or those unable to attend, may not fully grasp the complexities of publishing, distribution, printing, and royalty allocation. This challenge isn't unique to publishing. In any business, it's essential to seek and understand customer needs. Conversely, as a customer or author, sharing your needs is equally important. This type of communication fosters a thriving relationship where both parties create development and opportunities for each other.

# GIVING BACK: OUR PROUD SPONSORSHIP INITIATIVES

*"At the end of the day it's not about what you have or even what you've accomplished... it's about who you've lifted up, who you've made better. It's about what you've given back."*
–Denzel Washington

One of the achievements we take great pride in is our sponsorship program. To name a couple, we sponsor book festivals across the U.S. and host annual events for our author community. These events serve to market our authors, introducing them to a larger audience and connecting them with their brothers and sisters in authorship. At these events, we celebrate, entertain, educate, and create award-winning authors.

The success of these events depends heavily on effective communication. Just like organizing a wedding, ensuring we know who will be in attendance and that all attendees are informed is crucial for a smooth experience. Though perfection is what we seek, we are of the mindset that whatever happens, it was meant to happen. Our first conference lasted only three hours on a single day. By the second year, we expanded to a two-day event. Our third conference celebrated our three-year anniversary with a three-day event. It was so successful that we had to turn many people away while still accommodating unexpected guests.

Reflecting on this journey, I realize that dreams can indeed become reality. What started as a simple desire to help others share their stories has grown beyond my wildest expectations. It's important to celebrate the small victories, as they pave the way toward achieving your ultimate goals.

In addition to our annual events, we wanted to give back to our community, particularly to the youth who will shape our future. This led to the creation of The Little S}HE Project, another form of our community outreach. Through our annual events and our BNB Newsletter Mag sales, we raise funds to support young aspiring authors. The project encourages young girls and boys to pursue their writing dreams, creating valuable experiences for them. We're even in the process of implementing a summer and quarterly program for our young writers!

To date, we have raised funds for and published a few books through The Little SHE Project, including *Jordyn's Juvenilia*, *Shadow of Retribution*, and *Broken Crayons*. We have also collaborated with *Be the Miracle*, a nonprofit foundation, to implement a writing challenge. SHE PUBLISHING LLC will fund the winning project!!! We aim to make this an annual tradition.

So again, by attending our events and purchasing from our platform, you are not only enjoying quality entertainment, learning, and networking, but you are also supporting a noble cause. You are contributing to the success of our authors and investing in the future of our children.

# YOU KEEP CREATIVE CONTROL WHILE WE KEEP QUALITY CONTROL

*"Do something today that your*
*future self will thank you for."*
—Unknown

The publishing process is a collaboration between the author and the publisher. While the publisher is responsible for quality control, we ensure that authors retain their creative control. As previously mentioned, the information involved in the publishing process is extensive and cannot be conveyed in one sitting. Effective meetings typically last between 30 minutes to an hour, as attention spans wane and individuals can become overwhelmed beyond this duration.

Despite this, we often spend a considerable time addressing the unique needs of our authors, striving to cater to their individual requirements. Authors maintain creative control, and when it comes to reviewing the electronic proof, it is important for them to not only appreciate the appearance of the book but also to thoroughly read and review the accompanying instructions.

These instructions cover essential details, such as reminding authors to check for the latest changes being incorporated in the manuscript, identifying any spelling or grammatical errors, and verifying the ISBN to name a few. Additionally, the instructions highlight important considerations, such as the fact that electronic proofs should not be used to evaluate color or print quality. A physical copy should be reviewed for these aspects, as what appears on the screen may not accurately reflect the final printed colors.

It is important to note that if quality or professional photos are not submitted, the printed images may appear distorted. Some books are intentionally designed to look dated, and if that is the goal, the author and publisher must work together to achieve it. As the publisher, we will inform you if the absence of original pictures could impact print quality. But again, failing to review the instructions on the electronic proof can result in a low-quality final product.

Ultimately, the publishing process is a truly collaborative experience. A team is always stronger than an individual, and listening to the concerns of your team is invaluable. However, at the end of the day, the final decision rests with you.

The journey of publishing can lead to a rollercoaster of emotions – joy at seeing a book come to life, the challenges of trying to empower the author, along with what we think everybody wants; the constant tug-of-war between what the author truly desires vs. the desires of the author's readers.

I recall one of the authors posing a question: "*What do you do when you feel discouraged, overwhelmed, and you feel like giving up?*" At the time the author asked this question, I didn't have an answer, but if I knew then what I know now, I'd say:

*I am human. I am a believer; I am a woman; I am a mother; I am a daughter.... I hold many roles. I am prone to fatigue, doubt, and the occasional days where the mundane routines of life have felt like a suffocating blanket. But then, I think of the supportive people around me who loves me. I think of my daily blessings that we sometimes take for granted. I try to stay prayed up and I get my daily lessons by listening to Joel Olsten and other inspirational speakers. I dream of mornings spent with my kids, of afternoons filled with fitness and laughter, of evenings with family dinners and homework sessions. I dream of being an ATM for my daughter's entrepreneurial & college dreams, of being a better person, niece, and friend, traveling the world and being one of the best publishers I can be—aspiring to create projects better than I found them. So, this is what I do when I feel overwhelmed and discouraged. I have to identify those things that add to my emotional bank account.*

I credit the authors who are a part of the *She*Family who reach out occasionally, acknowledging and appreciating our efforts. They have been the light in the dark. It's those authors who continue to believe in SHE, who continue to believe in SHEnitha—a girl from humble beginnings who never imagined this passion would evolve into an extraordinary purpose. People remember how you make them feel first and foremost. This applies to both publishers and authors. It's a two-way street. Do you want people to avoid you because of your communication style, and reluctant to share information? Or do you want them to support you on your journey? People can unwittingly crush dreams with their words or actions, which is why I strive not to discourage those pursuing the dreams that have been given to them. It brings about great emotion to think that without starting this company, many wouldn't have this platform to share their stories or the patience to do so independently. Despite encountering discouragement, I press on, knowing the impact of my actions and understanding that this platform is not just for me, it is for the masses.

# FOSTERING RESPECT AND COLLABORATION LEADS TO AMAZING & CREATIVE PROJECTS

*"Collaboration equals innovation."* –Michael Dell

Over the years, I've learned how to effectively run this business, and I still have a lot to learn. My experiences have shown me the importance of protecting both our authors and our staff—the talented individuals who bring our projects to life.

I remember pairing an author with a staff member for a one-on-one collaboration, and it almost cost me the loss of that staff member due to the author's demanding behavior. While the author's vision drives the project, it is our staff who materialize that vision. Thus, it's crucial to approach the team who is supporting you with respect and understanding.

Although some might say, "I'm paying for this project, so it should be exactly how I want it and I will communicate how I want," know that it's important to realize that your approach significantly impacts the process. A positive and respectful approach can inspire and motivate, while a negative one can be detrimental.

I've found that encouraging the author and the supporting team by expressing confidence in their abilities fosters creativity and productivity. While the saying *"sticks and stones may break my bones, but words will never hurt me"* is often repeated, in reality, words can be deeply impactful. I see it all the time. Negative comments can overshadow numerous positive ones, affecting morale and performance.

My advice would be to assess any negative feedback, determine its validity, and make necessary adjustments while maintaining your passion. This mindset allows for each and every one of us to shine and produce our best work—remember, I am the publisher and the author.

After that experience, I decided to take on the role of a mediator to protect both the supporting team*she* and our author family. This ensures that our staff can work effectively, ultimately delivering a product that our authors will be proud of while they keep their creative control.

# "EMBRACING THE ENTREPRENEURIAL JOURNEY: CELEBRATING THE EFFORT AND VISION BEHIND EVERY BUSINESS"

*"The only impossible journey is the one you never begin."*
–Tony Robbins

With this being my final section of me confessing my experiences as a publisher, I'd like to say that I commend anyone who has the courage to step out on faith and start their own business. You should be proud of yourself. Whether your t-shirt business or brick and mortar is thriving, or if you had to close it due to overwhelming challenges, you embody the spirit of entrepreneurship.

Those who have never owned a business might not fully understand the immense hard work and long hours involved. When you work for someone else, you can clock out at the end of the day. But as a business owner, there are days when you work around the clock, taking only short naps, which is not healthy.

Your business, whether referred to as a hobby or a small venture by others, represents a significant achievement. Personally, I appreciate my 9 to 5 career because it enables me to pursue my 5 to 9 passion. Though the many roles I've held have been more mentally draining than physically draining, the satisfaction of building something of my own is unmatched.

From the onset of any business, you're often doing everything yourself. However, it's essential to recognize that you can't do it all alone, even in the beginning. As your business grows, securing a team to help you reclaim your time is crucial, allowing you to focus on your vision. I have a great team, but I also hire experts—graphic designers, editors, illustrators, and procedure writers—to handle areas where I may not excel. With this support, I can concentrate on what I love to do.

Some people might think that publishers get rich off publishing a single author's book, but that's not the case. There are countless hours of communication, strategizing, and marketing efforts behind the scenes. Authors often don't see half of the work a publisher does, but what I will continue to say to those who've done what I've done, embrace your entrepreneurial journey, learn from both the challenging and rewarding times, and remember that building a business is a remarkable accomplishment, deserving of recognition and respect.

# THIS IS OUR STORY

*From Projects to Publisher* is an invitation to every publisher, every entrepreneur, every soul chasing their own dreams. It's a reminder that the path to success is rarely paved with sunshine; it's a winding road, littered with potholes and detours. But with every challenge overcome, with every lesson learned, we inch closer to that elusive exit plan – a plan not just for financial freedom, but for personal fulfillment, for a life lived on our own terms.

This is my confession, aiming to influence both authors and publishers alike. It's a moment to step into my shoes, as I wear both hats—I am both the publisher and the author. Within my circle, I have friends who are publishers and friends who are authors. Fostering a sense of community within the broader community is key to the success of SHE PUBLISHING LLC. I want you to see the human side of this industry, the raw emotions, the triumphs, and the stumbles that make our journeys so relatable. I want you to understand that while the climb may be steep, the view from the peak is breathtaking.

So, hold onto your dreams, navigate the disappointments, and keep rewriting your own story—over and over again. The world needs your voice, your resilience, your unique blend of desires, decisions, and the occasional, inevitable, tantrum. This is your chapter, your confession, your roadmap to that ever-evolving exit plan. Write it with passion, with honesty, and with the belief that your story, just like a well-crafted book, deserves to be shared with the world.

# BONUS: THE LEGACY OF THE BOOK DRESS

In the third year of our anniversary, I envisioned a dress designed from books, symbolizing our commitment to literature and knowledge. With this vision in mind, I sought out Dress Mama of Lansing, Illinois, recalling her impeccable craftsmanship from creating my wedding gown.

Entering the store, memories flooded back as we reunited after some time apart. Recognizing her dedication to our publishing company's success, we embarked on a mission to JoAnn Fabric to procure the materials for this special garment. After a thorough search and assistance from a store clerk, we finally located the fabric.

A couple of days later, I eagerly returned to pick up the completed dress, knowing it would become my signature attire for all our events throughout the year 2023-24. This dress transcends mere fashion; it symbolizes the genesis of an enduring legacy. It is poised to become a piece for the company, etching its place in history and embodying the company's commitment to innovation and its trailblazing spirit.

So as we conclude our journey through this chapter and move on to the next, always remember: your story holds significance, and it's perfect with all of its imperfections.

# CHAPTER 9:

## BREAKING BOUNDARIES

*Becoming the Author of Your Story*

*"A day will come when the story inside you will want to breath on its own. that's when you'll start writing."* —**Sarah Noffke**

It's time to step out of the audience and onto the stage of your own life. No more watching others bask in the spotlight of their dreams; this chapter is your invitation to claim your own center stage, become the author of your story, and paint your masterpiece on the canvas of your existence.

Taking the assessment StrengthsFinder 2.0 reminds me that this isn't a one-size-fits-all kind of show. I've shared my personal blueprint for navigating some of my life's chapters with positivity. Now, it's time for you to pick and choose the elements that resonate with your soul, the tools that fit your toolbox, and create your own unique masterpiece.

This chapter is a distillation of the wisdom I've learned from navigating my own chapters, sprinkled with the collected goals and experiences of the talented authors who've journeyed alongside me. It's a map with small footprints of resilience; a compass guided by the star of self-belief.

I often emphasize the profound impact of exchanging inspirations within our author community, as it serves to strengthen our collective journey towards fulfilling our individual purposes. As you engage with the aspirations of our author family, I hope you find resonance and inspiration that propels you closer to embracing your own purpose and writing journey.

# GOALS OF OUR SHE PUBLISHING AUTHOR FAMILY

*"My goal is to be more active with my book in a sense of social and media presence. It's always been a little scary to put myself and my book out there, but I am proud of my work, so I think it deserves to be seen."* —**Khanyon G. Jerome, Author of Echo's Tale: Burden of the Tale**

*"My goal for 2024 is to reset my mind to being super courageous, bold, and exciting and to find creative ways to market and promote my books. Make the journey fun!!"* —**Licia Johnson, Author of I Am Fearfully and Wonderfully Made**

*"As an author, one of my goals is to get my work into the hands of more readers. One of the strategies I've decided to pursue is being more visible at vendor events. These events are great opportunities to connect with book lovers face to face, share my work, and build a community of readers who are interested in what I have to offer. This is the only way to ensure that my work is seen and appreciated by those who will genuinely enjoy it."* —**Dr. Calenthia Miller, Author of Unmask Series**

*"My author goal is to complete book II of "Making My Spirit Smile."* —**Tiffany Jackson, Author of Making My Spirit Smile**

*"To attend as many expos as possible in 2024 and to market Martell's World: You're No Different Than Me" to organizations to purchase my book in bulk."* —**Cynthia Green, Author of Martell's World**

*"Gain more exposure."* —**Royce Dixon Sr, Author of Hidden Feelings Revealed**

*"My goal as an author for next year is to inspire new generations of readers and for one of my novels to become award-winning books."* —**Marc A. Beausejour, Author of the BlackCyrano Series**

*"My primary goal is to complete the works that are currently in progress. Additionally, I've been tasked with writing a memoir biography about the life and enduring legacy of my father. I would like to improve marketing and distribution as well."* —**Dr. Samuel I. Brown, Author of Wounds Can Heal: Even If Scars Remain**

TO BETTER ALLOW PUBLIC AWARENESS about the book *"From My Eyes: Anchor Your Way to a Successful Elder Care Business,"* and its content." —**Shelita Woods, Author of From My Eyes**

*"To have lectures on my book through the county and in-depth panel discussions about the chapters."* —**Bobby McNeil Jr., Author of Cracking the Code**

# BEYOND THE MAP AND COMPASS

I want to offer you a quill – a powerful writing tool to help with your writing process. One of the most crucial steps we currently advise authors to take when beginning their writing journey is to attend the author's orientation and to utilize our SheWriter's Vision Planner. This invaluable tool provides authors with insightful writing tips and prompts to guide them along their path. The publishing process can be daunting, but the SheWriter's Vision Planner breaks it down into six manageable steps: selecting your publishing preference, drawing inspiration from your book cover, tackling where you are in the writing process, editing, formatting, navigating the publishing process, and finally, handling printing and shipping logistics.

Divided into three sections, the planner offers a structured approach: identifying goals and overcoming distractions, developing characters and crafting compelling narratives, and planning execution with yearly calendars. Whether an author is traditionally published or identifies as an indie author, the SheWriter's Planner offers practicality and seamless transition. However, just as in life, there may be roadblocks like the loss of a loved one or writer's block, or not enough time in the day; by focusing on the small steps, authors can steadily progress toward their larger publishing goals— one day at a time.

Remember, this isn't just about penning a bestseller (*although that's certainly no small feat!*); it's about the therapeutic act of storytelling itself. It's a journey of self-discovery, a mirror reflecting your strengths and vulnerabilities, and a dialogue with your inner spirit. Through the personal stories of our authors, we've witnessed firsthand the therapeutic benefits of putting pen to paper. One author bravely shares their experience of surviving sexual abuse, both by a neighbor and a family member. By channeling their pain into words, they found solace in expressing their emotions and reclaiming their narrative from the shadows of trauma.

Another author explores the struggle of masculinity, delving deep into their own journey of breaking down societal norms and embracing authenticity. For a soldier returning from war, writing became a means of processing the internal conflicts they faced upon reintegration into civilian life, ultimately sparking a call to action for protecting women and children within the communities. Amidst the chaos of the COVID-19 pandemic, one author recounts their harrowing experience of nearly losing their life to taking the shot, finding cleansing in documenting their journey towards recovery.

From the deeply personal topic of abortion to the professional setbacks of job rejections, from inspiring memoirs to children's books and/or poetry, each author found empowerment through sharing their stories, offering readers not only a glimpse into their lives but also a sense of connection and understanding. Through their words, they not only found healing for themselves but also became beacons of inspiration for others navigating similar challenges, proving that putting pen to paper and sharing one's truth with the world, really does make a difference.

And here's the beautiful truth: everyone has a story. Yours may not involve battling dragons or scaling corporate ladders, but it's a story, nonetheless. It's the tale of your laughter and tears, your triumphs and stumbles, your unique perspective on the ever-unfolding human drama. It's your fingerprint on the world, your contribution to the symphony of life.

Within our community of authors, diversity isn't just celebrated— it's cherished as the lifeblood of our collective stories. Each individual brings forth a distinct perspective, shaped by their unique experiences and cultural backgrounds. From stories of triumph over adversity to quiet moments of introspection, our authors transform ordinary experiences into extraordinary narratives that resonate deeply with readers, and through the pages of these stories, I encourage readers to embrace their own unique stories, recognizing the beauty beneath. After all, just as every person has a different thumbprint, so too do we each possess a story waiting to be told—an ordinary experience made extraordinary through the act of sharing it with the world.

As my mother mentioned in the foreword, I think of life as a playground—a vast, intricate game board, not unlike the iconic Game of LIFE that many have played with their families as children. We all start at the beginning, navigate squares of opportunity and adversity, and hopefully land on Park Place or Boardwalk with a satisfied smile. I'm sure we all remember that it's not just about the final destination; it's about the journey itself, the laughter shared with fellow players, the lessons learned from unexpected detours.

And finally, let's talk about the sweet reward of publication, the thrill of seeing your story transformed from whispers on a page to tangible proof of your existence. And as I say this, I'd like to add that publication is not the final chapter; it's merely a comma in the ongoing saga of your writing journey. So continue or begin to market your story, keep writing, keep sharing, keep breaking boundaries.

So, take a deep breath, and step onto the stage. Grab your pen, unleash your creativity, and start writing your own masterpiece, if you haven't already done so. The world awaits your unique symphony of experiences, woven into words that will resonate with hearts beyond your own. Again, this is not a solo performance; the stage is brimming with fellow storytellers, each with their own melodies to share. Join their chorus, harmonize your voices by creating anthologies, and create shared dreams and triumphs.

At the heart of our literary community lies a deep commitment to collaboration and support among our authors. Their encouragement and inspiration for one another throughout the writing and publishing journey is truly inspiring. Witnessing this firsthand, the camaraderie was visible during our author's orientation as they exchanged contact information and social media handles, eager to connect and amplify each other's voices. This selfless gesture speaks volumes about their character and dedication to lifting each other up. A profound understanding of the power of shared experiences and belonging fosters the very essence of SHE PUBLISHING LLC - we don't just publish books; we're building a community. Yearly interviews on the ShePub Network serve as a testament to this bond, showcasing not only book launches and relaunches, but also the enduring love and support within our community. In a world often characterized by division, this serves as hope for our collective future, rooted in collaboration over competition.

Just as my grandmother's belief planted the seed of SHE Publishing LLC, your story can inspire and empower others. It can become a lighthouse amidst the storms of doubt, a testament to the human spirit's unyielding capacity for courage. Imagine the ripple effect of your words, touching lives you never dreamt you could reach, igniting dreams you never knew existed.

As we journey across the U.S.A., our mission remains steadfast: to share the transformative power of our authors' books with readers around the globe. With each stop along the way, we've encountered more stories impact and heartfelt connection. In Houston, Texas, a young woman approached us, tears glistening in her eyes, to share how these stories have inspired her to share more and have helped her navigate the complexities of loss and grief, guiding her towards healing and acceptance. In D.C., a group of students eagerly discussed the insights they gained from another author's work, igniting passionate debates, and expanding their perspectives on societal issues. And in the Chicagoland area, we've gathered with our annual conferences to celebrate the words of every author on our roster, whose story of resilience inspired individuals facing adversity to find hope and strength within themselves. These are just a few glimpses of the countless lives as author and publisher. Our authors' books have touched the masses, illustrating the influence of their stories on readers from diverse backgrounds. As we continue to traverse the world, we carry with us the shared belief in the power of literature to foster learning, empathy, and positive change.

Every time you share your story, you chip away at the walls of indifference, reminding us that we are not alone in this grand experiment called life. So, let your voice ring out, unafraid and unfaltering. Let your vulnerabilities become your strengths, your imperfections, your brushstrokes of authenticity. The world needs your story, not a polished perfection, but a raw, vulnerable, and utterly human truth.

You are not a blank page; you are a canvas pre-filled with the vibrant pigments of experience. Take up your pen, dip it in the ink of your soul, and begin to paint your masterpiece. The world waits with bated breath, eager to witness the emergence of your unique tale. Now is your time to break boundaries, become the author of your story, and paint your life with the dazzling colors of your dreams.

Go forth and write your legacy. The stage is yours.

# CHAPTER 10:

## TURNING PAGES, INSPIRING LIVES

### The Family Operation

"Throughout my walk during this publishing process, I have found my "Boss Rules." God was carrying me and "Making My Spirit Smile" in the blessing of my storm as this relationship was being "Unveiled" right before my eyes. I wanted to win this "Spiritual War", so I looked through "Finch Files." I did all of this to maintain "A Sound Mind."
**—Shenitha Finesse Anniece**

This book may be a collection of chapters; but it's also a collection of our voices, a constellation of dreams made tangible on the page. It's a love letter to storytelling, and most importantly, a celebration of the authors who dared to turn blank pages into vibrant masterpieces.

Before I draw the final curtain on this journey, I want to turn the spotlight onto the very hearts that powered it - the team behind the scenes, and the authors who entrusted SHE PUBLISHING LLC with their precious words.

You'll meet authors who, once hesitant and unsure, found their confidence blossoming under the warm sun of this community. We'll hear summaries of their stories, diverse and compelling, each a testament to the power of finding one's own voice and sharing it with the world.

This chapter is a tribute to the author family of SHE PUBLLISHING LLC, and it will begin with a love letter to myself, a reminder that every journey starts with self-belief. This letter, inspired by Dr. Calenthia Yvette Miller writing her book "*A Love Letter to Ourselves*," an anthology of affirmations from around the world. This project encourages others to write a love letter to themselves. SHE Publishing LLC is the plant grown from the fertile ground of my own dreams. But like any seedling, it needed nourishment, and that sustenance came from the diverse and exceptional group of authors who graced my path. And my love letter goes like this:

*Dearest Self,*

*In the quiet spaces of my heart, I want you to know that I love you, even though I may not always show it. Your courage to embrace life in all its facets, to venture into the unknown unafraid of failure, has created the riches of experiences that life has bestowed upon you. If it were not for you being open to trying new things, you would not have become who you are today from projects to publisher and everything in between. Just know that you are still becoming.*

*I love you for daring to defy conventions, accepting your imperfections, and forging your own blueprint. I am grateful for your role as a follower, recognizing that it's the very essence that allows you to lead. The unbelievable thing is that people will follow you because they believe in you.*

*Your audacity to create, develop, and be your authentic self, letting your heart lead you to become your own beacon of inspiration. You have navigated through the diverse roles of life, and you don't always do it with grace. My only prayer is that you begin to take your health seriously and shower love on your family and friends because they are your pillars of strength; you need them. No one can survive in this world alone.*

*So I say to you, as you go into each new day, learn to love hard and build trust despite its challenges, because there is nothing like it. You will have stories to tell your children and grandchildren. Through the 3-ring circus, the engagement ring, the wedding ring, and the suffer-ring, you continue to keep him coming home with love, for now. Things can change in a split second.*

*Remember, everything you desire is attainable because you are His child. You are a cherished child by your father and mother, embraced by a divine love that knows no bounds. Remember what Terry said, "every day we are dying," so why not move mountains. You're an ordinary person who dreams of doing extraordinary things, so why not do it now. Continue to put out in the atmosphere what you desire and watch as it comes to life. Don't be afraid, call the banker for that building you desire. Don't be afraid. If not now, then when.*

*People are counting on you, so as you navigate the twists and turns, seize the reins of life with confidence, getting plenty of rest and water because it's not just about you, it's about all of His children, even the ones in your possession.*

*With boundless love,*

*Shenitha Finesse Anniece*

## the collection of
# SHENITHA FINEESSE
## ANNIECE

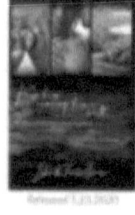

2020 | The Tribute to the Authors:

# Turning Voices into Legacies

Each year, a new wave of talent washed over the shores of SHE Publishing LLC, each author a unique vessel brimming with stories waiting to be shared. Starting with the 2020 class, these authors are truly built for beginnings. They taught me the courage to defy conventions and to have faith in who you are becoming every day.

# JORDYN'S JUVENILIA

## J. Lynniece
### THE SERIES

"Jordyn's Juvenilia" showcases drawings created by J. Lynniece from ages 5 to 9. Her passion for drawing was ignited by her struggles with communication and learning at the same pace as her peers. With the support of dedicated teachers, effective IEPs, and speech therapy, she is now on her way to liviing her dreams in color. Influenced by cartoons, movies, the Avengers, and the Disney Channel, her love for illustrating and creating toys blossomed.

J. Lynniece invites other children to join her project by coloring and writing their own stories surrounding her illustrations. Each child will have a unique story to tell! "Jordyn's Juvenilia" will feature many installments, and J. Lynniece is excited to collaborate with others in this creative and fun journey.

*To the author of Jordyn's Juvenilia*, you embody my Sherlock Holmes, my Einstein, and my Pablo Picasso all in one. You're my rainbow after the rain, my sun, my moon, my precious baby girl. You and your sisters hold the entirety of my world within you. There's nothing I wouldn't do for you. My love for you is immeasurable, beyond the reach of words. I want you and your sisters to recognize your incredible worth; you're all truly amazing. Your talent as an illustrator is unparalleled. You possess a remarkable gift, a discerning

eye that captures beauty effortlessly. Embrace every facet of your being, continue to express yourself boldly and creatively, and always maintain faith in your abilities. Know that I've learned invaluable lessons from you. Love you, later.

*Sharaka M. Leonard*

# BOSS RULES

## THE FIRST 25 STEPS TO INSPIRE YOU FORWARD

The intent *"Boss Rules"* is to inspire, open your mind to various perspectives, and affirm that you can be a BOSS right now. The first 25 steps to inspire you forward will reinforce the boss mentality and encourage you to be a boss because that is what you choose to be. Each rule provides advice for dealing with a belief or habit that can prevent people from fulfilling their dreams. It's like having your personal cheerleader to cheer you forward and support you on the journey.

Throughout most of the book, you will find real life examples and observations. The author also provides worksheets and contact information for one-on-one consultation at the end of this first volume to help readers transition from simply being inspired, to taking actual steps toward their goals. Give yourself the gift of accomplishment. Stop putting off what you can get started doing today.

*To the author of Boss Rules*, thank you for allowing me the opportunity to serve you. You are the marketing and mentoring guru who showed me the power of collaboration and the importance of tailored guidance. Your book continues to inspire me because it brings me back to the fundamental foundations of being a boss. Your books serves as a constant reminder that we all have unique paths to greatness.

*Tiffany Jackson*

# MAKING MY SPIRIT SMILE

## SEEING THE BLESSING IN THE STORM

Making My Spirit Smile is a memoir of a woman's life from infancy to young adulthood and chronicles the heartbreak and lack of love she experienced; it also highlights various moments when she felt God was with her, making her spirit smile even when she couldn't do it so outwardly.

In addition to sharing painful memories, the author encourages readers to find their own bright spots in dark times. She provides frank descriptions of mental, physical, and sexual abuse while also sharing ways in which she attempted to rise above and seek out safe spaces and helpful adults. Making My Spirit Smile is a self-aware read, and you will learn how she forgave at times as she reflects on the adults who inflicted harm upon her.

*To the author of Making My Spirit Smile*, and the recipient of the Janice Anderson Author Award, you've taught me the importance of nurturing relationships and staying positive even in the mist of the storm. You are the person who reminded me why I embarked on this journey: to empower voices like yours to reach the world. You remind me to stay humble and to be grateful for what I have and what I don't have. I encourage you to keep moving forward. As your next book blossoms, I can't help but feel the thrill of witnessing an award-winning author and speaker blossom. I carry your lessons of positivity close to my heart.

2021-23 | Beyond the Pages:

# A Ripple Effect of Inspiration

This journey wasn't just about publishing books; it was about igniting a chain reaction of hope and inspiration. Witnessing the impact of these authors' stories, the lives they've touched, the tears shed, the laughter shared – that knowledge filled me with a purpose beyond profit. It reminded me that every story and every voice holds the potential to build bridges of understanding and leave an indelible mark on the world.

# KODI

# BLACKMAN

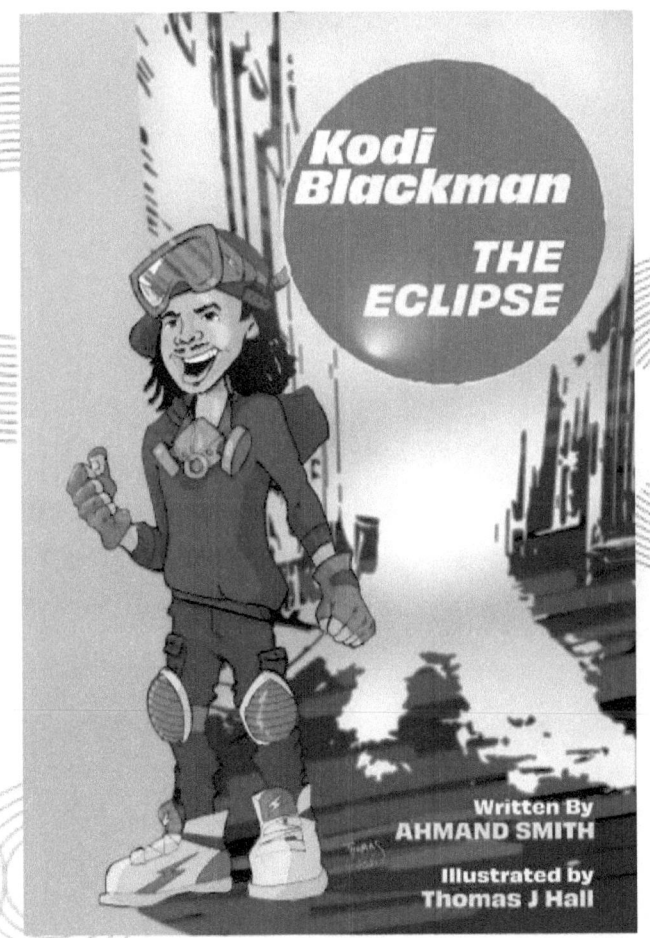

# Ahmand Smith

THE ECLIPSE

Kodi Blackman, an urban young man, begins working at RB Pest Solutions as an exterminator trained by an older wise man named Ol' Man Gym Shoe. Ol' Man Gym Shoe sparks the light shining through Kodi's fears and shyness, and he sees Kodi's innate superpowers, which represent the strengths found within all of our children.

As we experience Kodi's walk to gaining his self-confidence, the astounding illustrations will take us on a journey of Kodi's internal and external challenges, and the mysterious dreams of the King Moth that become a reality. These challenges will lead Kodi to achieve his faith, conviction, and ultimate success, empowering him to become his own hero.

*To the author of Kodi Blackman*, entrepreneur, and exterminator, you have created a masterpiece! You have been your own Kodi Blackman. You have inspired and encouraged children, the boys and girls characterized within numerous communities around the world, to decide to be their own superheroes. J. Lynniece was inspired by this book, and she became her own superhero! If you continue on, the books within this incredible series will educate and motivate our elementary and high school-aged children. You have also acquainted our adolescents with Kodi's unique career path while simultaneously bringing an out-of-the-box concept to create a new imaginary world of learning about the creatures we call bugs.

*Latosha Denise*

# UNVEIL
## A GUIDE FOR THE VOICELESS

UNVEIL, part memoir, part self-help, is a short read that includes snippets of a woman's abusive experience and the ten steps she takes to break free from the chains of domestic abuse. Latosha Denise reveals the chronicles of heartbreak, painful memories, and lack of love from the man she shared her world with and bears children with. The author briefly goes into how she'd consciously go in and out of another realm to escape the physical pain brought upon her, all while in the presence of her daughters. She was also shunned away from family and friends who encouraged her to make it work.

Latosha Denise acknowledges the moment she made the decision that enough was enough. She succeeded in removing herself and her daughters. Still, it wasn't until seven years later that Latosha Denise heard a familiar voice that brought upon anxiety, which would be the cause of her internal healing. She had yet to execute the one step placed in her heart.

While amid this storm, Latosha Denise formed a passion for helping others like herself, and she birthed Patricia's Place Domestic Violence Shelter: a secured facility and safe haven for women. So as you read this piece of her journey, it is with great intention that this self-help activity guide encourages readers to utilize ten steps to help them or someone in need to move beyond the inflicted pain of mental and physical abuse to a place of peace.

*To the author of Unveil*, your vulnerability became a mirror for countless readers, offering solace and strength in shared experiences. Thank you for believing in SHE to pull off this publication in 30 days. We met March 1st, and your book was published by March 31st with the collaboration and hard work of both of us. Thank you for sharing your personal space with me and my family. It is a true testament to the familial bonds that are created within our author family.

# PASTOR
# HENRY L. RAZOR

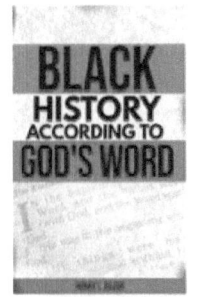
Released 1.1.2024

Released 5.11.2023

Releases 5.11.2023

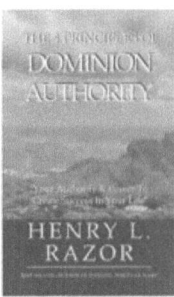
Released 11.25.2021

Released 12.25.2022

Released 1.1.2022

Released 3.9.2021

**Winning Spiritual Wars: Unleashing the Power of the Soul! by Henry L. Razor** | This book begins by explaining the biblical command to strategize and prepare for war in the Spiritual World. It also answers the question of why we have to fight in the 'Spiritual World' and provides a biblically sound and scripturally supported explanation for the creation of our enemy. Pastor Razor explains how, in the very make-up of humans, God has prepared us to be victorious against our spiritual enemies.

This book takes us through very detailed explanations of the parts of man and the role each part has in Spiritual Warfare. A four-step biblical *'best practice'* for winning wars against spiritual enemies is then put forth in detail with supporting scriptures. This book concludes by analyzing Jesus' successful use of this four-step method.

Terms such as *'Spiritual Sponsors'* and the *'dual citizenship'* of man are introduced and defined. This book is an asset for all Christians facing sickness, poverty, depression, or any form of spiritual opposition; and should be in every Christian's library. This book will produce results in Spiritual Warfare that will manifest in your natural life. Your life will improve!

**"Black History According to GOD's Word"** by Pastor Henry L. Razor asserts that Black History began with Adam's creation, as revealed in the inspired word of God. Pastor Razor explores scriptural indications of a predominantly black global population and traces migratory paths from Eden, demonstrating the vital role of Black People in establishing civilization. Beyond scripture, the book integrates insights from respected scientists. It concludes by emphasizing the significance of this knowledge for believers, offering a comprehensive resource for classrooms, churches, and conferences. Each enlightening chapter unveils the pivotal role of

Black People in God's plan for the world, making it an essential read for all, particularly those of faith."

**"The Four Principles of Dominion Authority Your Authority & Power to Create Success in Your Life"** by Henry L. Razor is a booklet that introduces you to four valid principles. These principles are to desire it, speak it, believe it, and act upon it, whatever that it is for you. Razor reminds us that implementing the laws of dominion authority has the power to force change at a personal level in your life as you begin to utilize these principles and by applying them in accordance with our usage of this law.

**Biblically Black & Blessed What the Bible Says About God's Relationship with Black People** by Henry L. Razor | WHAT DOES THE BIBLE SAY ABOUT GOD'S RELATIONSHIP WITH BLACK PEOPLE? The best-selling author of Winning Spiritual Wars Unleashing the Power of the Soul, by Pastor Henry L. Razor, has relaunched Biblically Black & Blessed.

Through a detailed and careful analysis of the Bible, Pastor Henry Razor explains his interpretation of God's relationship with Africans and those of African descent while revealing God's functional assignment for the descendents of Noah's son Ham. This book begins the relationship analysis with the creation of man and continues it to date.

**Biblically Black & Blessed II The Children of the Ethiopians by Henry L. Razor** | The best-selling author of Winning Spiritual Wars Unleashing the Power of the Soul, by Pastor Henry L. Razor, has launched Biblically Black & Blessed II The Children of the Ethiopians on Christmas Day. This holiday release intends to reveal Razor's complete interpretation of Galatians 3:28

*"There is neither Jew nor Greek, there is neither bond nor free, there is neither male nor female: for ye are all one in Christ Jesus."*

Understanding how God relates to the children of the Ethiopians has been the most enlightening and eye-opening Bible knowledge that

Razor has acquired in the 50+ years since Missionary Banks/Sanders walked him through the doors of the Earle COGIC. To have this kind of understanding is essential because it emphasizes the biblical fact that God does not view any group of people, or any ethnic nationality, to be better than, more important than, or superior to any other group of people on this earth.

It has been stated that the best way to understand the Bible is to let it explain itself. So, grab your copy of Biblically Black and Blessed II so we can attain this understanding together.

**Your Purpose is Your Superpower Discover Your Life's Assignment and Become a Powerful You (The Workbook)** by Henry L. Razor | This workbook is produced and intended to accompany the ' Your Purpose is Your Superpower Discover Your Life's Assignment and Become a Powerful You ' book. It can be effectively used in workshops, conferences, and seminars. Although the process and procedures outlined in this book have a history of effectiveness and success, no guarantee is made pertaining to the usage and application of these principles because personal adherence to and compliance with these guidelines and principles are not assessed, validated, or verified; neither is there ever any attempt to assess, validate, or verify. Faith varies and is individual and personal, and as such, so are the results of applying the principles of this workbook. At the completion of this workbook, the participant should be able to: state why knowing your purpose is critical for life's success, list three ways in which we discover our purpose, and apply the content and biblical structure presented in this seminar to your life to arrive at what God has placed you on this earth to do.

*To the author of the Holiday Series*, the best-selling award-winning author, the recipient of the Janice Anderson Author Award and the Triple Threat Award, thank you for your constant prayers and spiritual guidance as it has been the light for all of the authors on this roster. You and your family exemplify the true meaning of support and love. Thank you for believing in SHE from day one and for being an integral part of our journey. Your faith and dedication inspire us every day!  Know that what you do and have done been the world to us!

# stacie p. calvin

# A SOUND
# MNND
## THE REBIRTH

**A Sound Mind: The Rebirth** is a memoir about a woman's journey of re-finding herself after experiencing a life-changing adventure. Was this all just a dream, or was this a reality? It came to the point where others had to intervene and take ownership in helping to resolve this unforeseen challenge.

Stacie P. Calvin is in full bloom, and in this story, she gives us the treat of several inspirational quotes, acronyms, and things that helped her throughout this voyage. Calvin realizes that her inner satisfaction, her truth, ultimate fulfillment, purpose, and true happiness will never be fully unlocked until she unleashes her unique gift that will resolve the world's unique need. She shares the four promises that we must claim to our path of having a sound mind.

As you read, you'll begin to see the revelation of spoken words come to fruition. So get ready for an adventure while you are taken on a journey; the journey of a resilient woman manifested. **A Sound Mind: The Rebirth**.

*To the author of A Sound Mind*, you remind me that blood is thicker than water, but you need water to survive. You are the reason I keep moving forward. You've shown me that I can have true love and care for the people I serve. I love you and I mean it.

*Antonius E. Finch*

# FINCH FILES

## SHORT STORIES FROM A CHI-TOWN ENGLEWOOD BLOGGER

Antonius "Smooth" Finch is a Chi-Town blogger who's put together a series of short stories into a book. These short stories are an inspiration of originally written blogs that outline his experiences, viewpoints, successes, and pain while living in the Englewood area of Chicago, Illinois.

Mr. Finch certainly has provided us with a variety of topics that will intrigue us. He even allows us the option to comment on the various issues that may be controversial. You can look forward to reading about his views on men in relationships, the NFL, the Love Experience, domestic violence, the pursuit of happiness, and so much more.

*To the author of "Finch Files,"* the award-winning author of Black Authors Matter TV, and my Curie Condor classmate, your work has reminded us to value the lesson of time. You emphasize the importance of recognizing those who surround us, and that success starts with investing in our own communities. Your passion for giving back is truly inspiring. Thank you for allowing us the opportunity to serve you and for your continued support. We are grateful to have you and the other authors as a part of the *She* family.

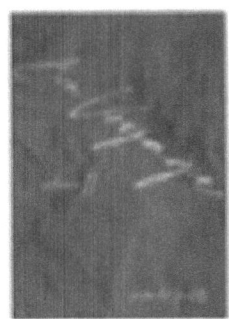 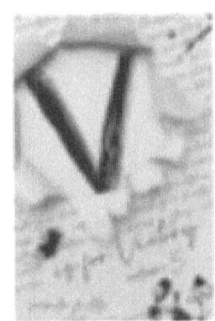 

# *Pamela* FIELDS

## THE POETRY SERIES

Buckle your seat belts as you are presented with 50 poems written in the error of the COVID-19 pandemic. Fields shares her diagnosis and prescription through her art of poetry, encouraging hope and persuading the act of man to change their mindset during these trying times.

*Veto My Vote*, by Pamela Fields, is volume twelve of a collection of poems charged and fueled with purpose, progression, and power; hence why this volume was released, superseding volumes four through eleven.

In this book, you will begin with Life's Lessons, Precious Pearls, The Price of Sin, and the Author of Life, to name a few. Take the time during intermission to reflect on what's been shared. After that, you will continue with Once Upon a Time, Hounds at my Feet, I Want to Live, and more poetry to pique your interest in its conclusion.

Veto My Vote | Volume Twelve is an attestation that your mindset contributes to your ambition to not only survive in this life but to live.

*Building A Village* is another empowering poetry book of 50 poems revealing the continuation of manifestation, healing, hope, self-love, revelation, reflection, free, inner-strength, and grace. You are sure to find a connection to a few, if not many.

Fields again share the prescription of hope and her continued journey through the art of poetry. You will begin with To My Sons, Purpose of Struggle, A New Focus, A Spirit of Midnight, and Lifeguard, to name a few.

Take the time during intermission to reflect on what's been shared. After that, you will continue with The Best Teacher, A Sketch of

Beauty, Portrait of a Servant, Shallow Waves, and many more to pique your interest in its conclusion.

*Again, Building A Village | Volume Three* is the third book to a series of poetry books by Pamela Fields, a woman's collection of expressions from experiences, a woman who wears many hats. This poetry book and the others to come is an attestation that your pain contributes to your ambition to be a testament to someone who may share the same struggles and desires.

*Vitamins of Hope*, by Pamela Fields, is another empowering poetry book of 50 additional poems that reveal the continuation of manifestation, healing, hope, self-love, revelation, reflection, free, inner-strength, and grace.

Fields share the prescription of hope, sharing her continued journey through the art of poetry. You will begin with A Forgotten Commodity, Words of Flavor, and Intricate Webs of Life, to name a few. Take the time during intermission to reflect on what's been shared. After that, you will continue with Success, Have You Ever, Amalikites, and many more to pique your interest to its conclusion.

Vitamins of Hope | Volume Two is the second book to a series of poetry books by Pamela Fields; a woman's collection of expressions from experiences, a woman who wears many hats. This poetry book, and the others to come is an attestation that your pain contributes to your ambition to be a testament to someone who may share the same struggles and desires.

*A Positive Version*, by Pamela Fields, is an empowering poetry book of 50 poems that reveal manifestation, healing, hope, self-love, revelation, reflection, freedom, inner-strength, and grace. It also touches on death, heartbreak, pain, sadness, questions, bondage, anxiety, and loneliness. You are sure to find a connection to a few, if not many.

As Fields shares her journey through her poetry Little Children, A Prayer in My Pocket, You Turn, Chocolate Blood, Cries of the City, Marriage on the Rocks, to name a few, take the time during intermission to reflect on what's been shared. After that, you will continue with Somewhere Betwinx, Faces, Real Men's Tears, Expectations, My Soul Longeth, and many more to pique your interest to its conclusion.

A Positive Version is the first book to a series of poetry books, a woman's collection of expressions from experiences, a woman who wears many hats. This poetry book, and the others to come, is an attestation that your pain contributes to your ambition to be a testament to someone who may share the same struggles and desires.

Ultimately, Field's purpose and passion are to bring together ordinary people like you and me with the commitment to encourage us to love one another. She believes that it's the small efforts of a friendly smile, the gift of gratitude, praying for one another, and small acts of kindness that will change the world one day, one hour, and one second at a time. It only takes a second to yield a smile and patience doesn't cost anything.

There's more poetry books in the making…

*To the author of the poetry series,* poetry becomes you and you remind me of my grandmothers' kind heart. You've graced the cover of the BNB newsletter mag you are a 2x Triple Threat Award Winner, so keep moving forward. It's time for people to know who you are. You remind me to continue to be resilient and that there is a true power in forgiving.

*Micah & Torri*

# GORDON

## ONE TO WON

**One To Won: Strategies to being a Power Couple that wins at Life and Love** by Micah and Torri Gordon | Are you wondering what's wrong with your relationship? Have you felt like giving up? Do you want better for you and your significant other? If you can honestly say yes to these questions, you've picked the right book.

Micah and Torri Gordon have spent over 10 years together loving, learning, and building a life to support others through mentoring and counseling. They are sharing those lessons here with unprecedented honesty and hopeful encouragement. This powerful couple knows that a strong foundation is necessary to build a beautiful life, and they have dedicated themselves to helping others begin or continue their journeys with love. Whether you are single and looking to find a partner or are already a couple looking to expand your impact, this book is for you.

*To the authors of One to Won,* your book demonstrates the commitment you both have to being an advocate for marriages. Thank you for allowing us to collaborate in the relaunch of your book. Your collaborations in *One to Won* showcased the beauty of diverse perspectives. And to one of the greatest singers I know, Torri, you were a ray of sunshine at our first conference. I wish you both the very best. Please continue to pave the way for successful marriages.

# KIM MATTEAR

*My Poems*

# OF VIEW

*MY POEMS OF VIEW* is a collection of poetry by the author and artist Kim Mattear. She takes you on a journey throughout her life which includes her successes and challenges, the love of her parents who are watching from the heavens, relationships with friends, adornment of her siblings, love, relationships, and much more. You will begin her journey by reading *Another Day*, *Between the Two*, and *Guess Who*? Continuing with *It Gets Lonely*, *Life's Blues*, and *REALADY*. *And if you haven't had enough,* conclude with *Who Said*, *Women Who Love Too Much*, and *You Know What to Do*. There are so many more poems in between!

These poems were created years ago, and as Mattear began to bring this dream to a *Reality*, she began to relive what she'd encountered during her journey through life. This experience has brought tears and discomfort at times but has become a form of healing. Although Mattear started writing two other books, she constantly heard the voice to move forward with the release of *My Poems of View*. And now, as you read this book description, it has come to fruition. The doors of opportunity have opened yet again, and Mattear took that leap of faith. She now presents the 164-page book of poetry. The stars have aligned.

As you begin to read, you'll notice the different styles used to write this poetry. It resembles a mixture of short stories and experiences in poetry form. So, place yourself in Mattear's shoes as she captures your attention with the bold headers and vibrant images within *My Poems of View*.

*To the author of My Poems of View*, the CEO of Golden Publishing (*a sister publishing company to SHE*), I will never forget how we met. You reached out to me and when I tried to return your call, you thought it was a scam. You damn near cursed me out, but the moment you realized I was the publishing company you reached out to, you were so apologetic and from that very day, we talked on the phone for about an hour plus, and you became my sister, literally; Golden Publishing LLC. Thank you for always being a ride or die supporter of your family in SHE. So much so that when you started Golden Publishing LLC, you promoted all of the sister companies on your website. You never forgot how this relationship started. I remember meeting you in-person for the first time at the first annual SHE CONFERENCE and networking convention. It was a 3-hour event, which has now turned into a multiple day event. I remember you were dealing with a family situation, and you took a moment to take my call. That is the type of love that keeps me inspired and moving forward. I thank you for treating me like your real sister in love.

Shartia
LOVE JONES

THE BUTTERFLY SERIES

**The BUTTERFLY Series** by Shartia "Love" Jones, Prayers for You Child from Head to Toe, Overstanding the Game, and Daddy's Girl.

*Prayers for Your Child from Head to Toe* is an interactive prayer book for our children power packed with scripture, prayers, and reflective journaling sections. Jones wants you to read and enjoy the morning and bedtime prayers. The journaling sections will allow parents to share their input, thoughts, feelings, and emotions. It will foster a safe space enabling the opportunity to write your specific prayers from the heart, the personal prayer for your child(ren). The best part of this book is to reflect on the moment your prayers are answered.

*Overstanding the Game* | Coming Soon!

*Daddy's Girl* | Coming Soon!

*To the author of the butterfly series*, the genuine voice of SHE, the nominee of the Janice Anderson Author Award, your contribution has been grand in our growth. Your unwavering belief and trust in the *She*family philosophy has been instrumental, and with your encouraging words, Latoya and Marc are now a part of our author family. It's important for me to acknowledge those who played a crucial role in forging connections throughout this journey—and you were one of those precious people. Words fail to express how much you mean to SHE. You're more than just an author; you're my companion in travel, and you've evolved into someone I consider a friend.

*Pamela*

# JAMES COLEMAN

## THE SERIES

**Vengeance: Justice's Revenge by Pamela James Coleman** | "I was climbing back to the street when I saw the women from my past and present standing at the top of the hill. At first, I was happy to see them all there, that meant that they still cared about me, right? As I continued back up the ditch," he starts again with the heavy coughing, "I started to think about how I got down here. Are they here to make sure I am, ok? Or are they here to make sure I died? I rolled back down the hill. I crawled into a drain until the police and firefighters left the area."

"I will handle this on my own."

"I am going to take care of them one at a time!"

**Is this me? Am I her?** is a chronicle of Pamela James Coleman's roller coaster ride of life events. Coleman will take you through the good moments she experienced as a child growing up, which were shadowed by drinking, mental abuse, drugs, and lies. As you read, you will meet family members who did their best to protect her. You will see how living around alcoholism influenced and affected some, if not all, of Coleman's choices.

Growing up, Coleman always wanted the life of the families seen on the television. She yearned for a mother-daughter relationship. Neither was meant to be. Her doctor suggested visiting a psychiatrist, but the money was tight. Not to mention, doctor visits were not in the budget either. So instead, James put pen to paper to express her feelings, and this book became a healing process for James. This book is divided into three chapters, sharing the good times and the bad. James's goal is to show how an individual can go through the darkest times and still come through it stronger and wiser.

As the conclusion of this book, Coleman stands alone in an empty house, looking forward to finding herself and leaving you in suspense. James continues to ask herself, "Is this me? Am I her?

**Finding Herself...I Was Not Her!** by Pamela James Coleman, takes the reader through the loss of a husband, the loss of a grandmother, legal issues resulting from the grandmother's care, and employment issues that largely resulted from the legal issues. You will gain a distinctive point of view; although these problems are not unusual in and of themselves, Pamela will give us an idea of what it was like for you as an individual to experience them. And that's the value of a book like this-this is not merely a story about someone who experiences these setbacks and gets through them; this is the story of a real person who pops off the page and gives you hope regardless of your circumstances. With that said, buckle your seat belt and be ready to cry, laugh, and experience the journey of life through the eyes of Pamela James Coleman as she finds herself.

*To the author of this series*, an award-winning author, indie and published author, you are doing amazing things. I love your determination. Not only are you taking the world by storm, but you demonstrate how to use your resources and to promote your dreams. Your influence on this platform is multifaceted and inspiring. Not only have you encouraged everyone to explore and step out of their comfort zones through travel, but you've also taken the lead in presenting the men's mental health seminar. Your achievements are remarkable, and your determination is truly admirable. Beyond making waves globally, you're affecting real change in the lives of men and actively supporting the mental health movement. Personally, you continue to teach me the significance of determination, dedication, and self-belief.

THE
POWER
OF YOU,
NO ONE
IS YOU
AND
THAT IS
YOUR
POWER!

**The POWER of You! No one is YOU, and that is your POWER!**

IGNITE YOUR *PASSION* | DISCOVER YOUR *PURPOSE* |
STEP INTO YOUR **POWER!**

Get ready to be Em**POWER**ed as **POWER**house author, speaker, trainer, and veteran real estate trusted advisor, Bertina Power, takes you on a journey to uncover the **POWER** that lies within you. Bertina's energetic, authentic, and electric delivery style shines through as she gives you the blueprint to activate your internal POWER source. When the storm hits, many of us want to run and hide, blame others for our misfortune, or cry out, 'Why me?" From mindset to resources, from words to forgiveness, **The POWER of You!** provides the tools needed to access your strengths, release your maximum potential, and unlock your **POWER**.

Every person has a hidden **POWER** source waiting to be activated, and Bertina Power, a certified and bona fide **POWER** igniter is the right woman for the job! Be forewarned: after reading this book, your life will be forever changed. Be prepared to experience a heightened hunger for success! You will become unrecognizable as you discover…

**No one is YOU, and that is your POWER!**
I am writing this letter to highly recommend Bertina Power for her outstanding contributions and leadership at SHE PUBLISHING LLC. Since joining our publishing company as an author in 2022, Bertina has demonstrated exceptional qualities that set her apart as a true leader and inspiration to others.

*To the author of The Power of You! No One is You and That is Your POWER*, an award-winning best-selling author, if I could write a recommendation, it would start something like this: Bertina's commitment to excellence and active participation have been evident in her role at SHE PUBLISHING LLC. Not only has she achieved the remarkable feat of becoming a two-time bestseller, but she has also been the driving force behind the creation and introduction of the innovative *She*Experience publishing package. Her ability to recognize and leverage available options, coupled with her creative thinking, has significantly enriched our publishing offerings.

There is certainly much more to say in your recommendation. You have become a regular presenter at our annual conferences, generously sharing your knowledge and experiences with a wider audience. Your insights and expertise have significantly enhanced the quality of our events, making them even more valuable for attendees.

When we were preparing for our second annual conference and Mama*She* was unavailable, you stepped in, covering the chairs and working your magic decorating the podium. We have so many shared memories, and I deeply appreciate your contributions.

Thank you for welcoming me and my family into your personal and historical space. By the way, I think you should have a shrimp taco fiesta while empowering the youth—*hint, hint*!

PEPPERMINTS AND ROSES

**PEPPERMINTS and ROSES** by Jonathan Jefferson | As a prelude to the release of '*Just life,*' '*Peppermints and Roses*' takes a peek into the heart and soul of the author and creative writer Jonathan D. Jefferson. Influenced by his belief in God and experiences traveling 13 countries (*and counting*), including Iraq, Kuwait, South Africa, and Thailand. The book is an artistic portrayal of life seen through the windows of the author's soul. Many pieces, such as '*Letter to a Black Soldier*' and 'Good Morning' express a unique and personal perspective displayed without the filter of perceived norms or accepted generalizations. Every experience in life is holistic in that each person's thoughts, feelings, emotions, and reactions are from a different point of view. Filled with the good, bad, and shared experiences we live. We are similar as well as diverse, like Peppermints from Venus and Roses from Heaven.

*To author of Peppermints and Roses* who share my birthday, and to one of the most remarkable poets I've encountered, your words demand to be heard. Your journey across the globe, including encounters with mortality, lends a depth to your poetry that resonates profoundly. Among your works, my personal favorite is *A Black Soldier*. Your book served as the catalyst for our incorporation of living roses into the custom boxes for our readers, alongside peppermints, as a symbolic representation of its essence. Moreover, your clear vision for the aesthetic of your book prompted us to expand our roster of graphic designers. Some authors join us with precise visions, and you were one such visionary, which again, led us to discover a talented new graphic designer. Your understanding that our events are not solely the company's but also your own underscores your deep involvement and commitment to our collective journey.

PHOENIX TRANSFORMING

**Phoenix Transforming | From Ashes to Ascension** by Lesa Butler is the story of one woman's journey from ashes to ascension, from darkness to sunlight, from bondage to freedom. After a decade-long battle with PTSD resulting from childhood and adult trauma, Lesa shares how she rises out of the soot and into flight. Lesa takes the reader through the steps she implemented to aid in her healing and restoration. She wants the reader to know that no matter how far down into the dirt he or she falls, ascension is possible!

Lesa Butler is an author, ghostwriter, educator, and speaker born and raised in Chicago, Illinois.

Lesa's purpose and passion lie in assisting others in healing while helping to bring their dreams to fruition. She does this through ghostwriting, book development, workshops, and speaking.

*To the author of Phoenix Transforming,* you are one of the most talented writers I've encountered. If writing is your passion, I wholeheartedly encourage you to continue pursuing it. As a publisher, I understand how the weight of others' expectations and demands can sometimes become overwhelming. However, I urge you to keep moving forward and pressing on. Don't let anyone sabotage your aspirations—no one is perfect.
I've come to appreciate the importance of transformation, much like the unyielding cycle of growth shown by an eagle. Your influence within our company is profound, and you will remain in our thoughts and prayers.

HISTORY AND CONTRI- BUTIONS OF THE BLACK WOMAN FROM PAST TO PRESENT

ELOGEIA HADLEY

**Who Is She? History and Contributions of the Black Woman from Past to Present** by Elogeia Hadley is a historical nonfiction read dedicated to black women who have been the sheroes, influencers, queens, and warriors of their time. The revelation of this read shines the light on black women who made contributions to our society that should be celebrated. Hadley introduces you to 50 black women you may or may not know. The progression of this story is in divine order as she begins with historical facts about one of the oldest females ever found in Africa and continues with revealed stories of women from all over the world. Hadley concludes this read with women of the present; women who partake in candid conversations and "Sista-to-Sista" moments.

In the story Who Is She? Hadley shows the world that Black African women are the beginning, they gave birth to the world as we know it. Take this journey of getting to know black women of the past and the present, and gain the answer to the question, Who Is She?

*To the author of Who Is She*, thanks to you, I've had the privilege of crossing paths with someone who has become a sister to me, despite not sharing the same bloodline. Your influence has ignited a passion within me to explore the remarkable stories of women throughout history, particularly those of African American descent. "Who Is She" stands as a testament to the importance of celebrating the journeys and achievements of women like us.

Your drive and accomplishments serve as a constant source of inspiration for me. Your ability to achieve what many only dreams of is nothing short of remarkable. Securing your own rental space is a significant milestone, and I couldn't be happier for you.

I can't help but imagine the impact you could have by penning a book that celebrates the trailblazing African American women of our time. Your unique perspective and experiences could forge a new chapter in history, inspiring generations to come. And I look forward to you becoming a sister company, if this is something that you desire.

Exquisite Egyptian Belly Dance Moves
Fun • Fitness • Femininity

Khalidah Kali

EXQUISITE EGYPTIAN
BELLY DANCE MOVES

# LICIA JOHNSON

# I AM

# FEARFULLY

# *and wonderfully* MADE

**I Am Fearfully & Wonderfully Made by Licia Johnson** | *I Am Fearfully and Wonderfully Made*, a children's book by Licia Johnson, focuses on the relationship of two sisters and touches on issues related to womanhood and coming of age. The three primary characters in this story are Makayla, Mona, and their mother. The author provides personal details to build Makayla's character early on. The relationship between the sisters is a driving force throughout the work, transitioning from strained to strong. Although the sisters initially do not get along, both of them experience trying times that ultimately serve to bring them closer together. The most important part of this story is that Makayla finally realizes that she is *Fearfully and Wonderfully Made*!

*To the author of I Am Fearfully and Wonderfully Made*, you have taught me that it is okay to be vulnerable. You are enough. All of your books have been a form of therapy for you. You have shared some of your most personal and private moments with the world and I admire you for that. Let's continue to showcase your work. Join some book tours, keep moving forward and your dreams and aspirations will come true.

# IVA MARTENEZ

new title
COMING SOON!

# Gregory D. Davis

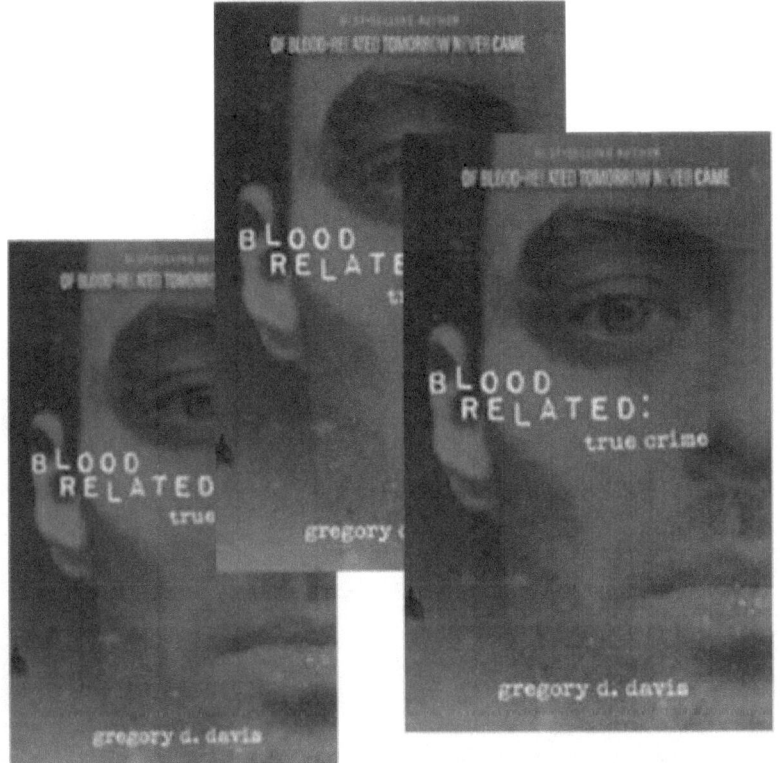

blood related
TRUE CRIME
BEST-SELLING AUTHOR OF
TOMORROW NEVER CAME

**Blood Related: True Crime by Gregory D. Davis** | Gregory D. Davis, best-selling author of Blood Related | Tomorrow Never Came, presents us with **Blood Related | True Crime**. Blood Related | True Crime is a fictionalized true-crime story about a bizarre case in Arkansas where the directors of a failing funeral parlor hired a killer to drum up business. The story's backdrop is the sleepy community of Pampa County, Arkansas, located in the Delta Region, with a population of less than five thousand. It was a relatively poor community, but they all stuck together and treated each other like family. As time would have it, many young progressive folks went off to college or the military. Eventually, they started their lives in other states, only returning for some holidays, funerals, or any different life-changing family situations.

Faith and Grace Calhoun had genuine intentions of trying to save the family business until their plans skyrocketed out of control. They never imagined the far-reaching impact their choices had on the lives of their beloved community. They were known throughout the County as Wilson Calhoun's girls who had everything they ever wanted. He had their lives all planned out where all they had to do was do the right thing, go to college, graduate, and find good jobs. They accomplished those goals set by their father's guided plan but decided to go off their life's script and add their own goals, which would prove to be as they could have ever imagined.

You will be intrigued as this gripping tale of a roller coaster ride will keep you on the edge of your seat from beginning to end. You will get to know the residents of Pampa County, who receive roomy portraits before they lock into their places in the plot. This book is a page-turner, one that will surely keep you on your toes and will make it difficult to put down. Hold onto your hats and buckle up for the suspenseful ride of your life!

*To the brilliant mind and best-selling author of "Tomorrow Never Came,"* you are among the most imaginative fiction writers of our time. Your stories deserve to be heard and, in my vision, adapted into films. Thank you for giving us the privilege to publish your second book. We eagerly anticipate your future works. Additionally, we appreciate your referrals, which have led to the addition of two new authors to our family. We are honored to feature you on the cover of the upcoming Books -N- Business Newsletter Magazine—congratulations!

# Chantell Windham

*I Had Cancer, Cancer Never Had Me* **by Chantell Windham** takes the reader on a journey through the Stage 2 Breast Cancer experience of Chantell Windham. This thought-provoking work chronicles the reactions and effects of her diagnosis on those closest to her. Along with detailed accounts of the responses of friends and loved ones, the author also includes key life lessons learned throughout her journey.

*I Had Cancer, Cancer Never Had Me* is a blended presentation that will make you laugh, cry, and crave more information. Chantell's story of love, sacrifice, and triumph over a seemingly uncomfortable giant is sure to move you in unexpected ways. The author's view of her breast cancer Journey as a celebration rather than a curse reminds us of all the power of perspective.

*To the author of this amazing book read,* your courage to write your story has been such an inspiration. The way that this book takes us through your days of sharing the news with your family taught me that with the support of family, anything is possible. If I could give you a nick name, it would be ***strength***.

# S.R. Mays

THE
**EFFECTIVE**
USE OF
**SPIRITUAL**
**TOOLS**

S.R. MAYS

*opioid*
# ADDICTION
FINDING A WAY OUT

*The Effective Use of Spiritual Tools*, a self-help read by S.R. Mays describes the spiritual tools used by the author to overcome substance abuse and addiction, and it encourages us to live a full, spiritual life. The author does a good job presenting what worked for him to overcome his opioid addiction. Mays explains his recovery process clearly and uses plenty of clear examples to illustrate his points.

Mays is grounded in his faith; his passion shows clearly through the words on these pages. In addition, he explains how he used the tools he presents throughout this story; spiritual tools such as meditation and prayer. The author's goal is to help others to discover the tools they have in their very own possession and how those spiritual tools can work for them. Mays overcame the struggle, and so can you!

*To the author of The Effective Use of Spiritual Tools*, thank you for your vulnerability and for sharing your story. Your interview on the ShePub Network was eye-opening, offering insights on handling major life challenges and addressing how families can support loved ones battling opioid addiction. You are a valuable member of our literary family, and we thank you for allowing us to serve you.

# Felecia Portwood

*the cost of*
# DISOBEDIENCE
WHAT PRICE WILL YOU PAY

**The Cost of Disobedience : What Price Will YOU Pay** by Felecia Portwood | Inspired by a true story, *The Cost of Disobedience | What Price Will You Pay?* by Felecia Portwood takes you on a journey of an adult woman who gets involved with a man who happens to have met her at the perfect hour of a very heated evening. Their relationship ultimately leads to a marriage that affords her many valuable necessities of life. This story captures her struggles to be a good wife and mother, maintaining love, peace, and happiness while enduring deceit, adultery, abuse, disrespect, manipulation, control, and division from her loved ones.

This story begins on the south side of Chicago in 2004 when after multiple failed relationships, a woman tries to find peace and live a drama-free life, not knowing the drama awaiting her ahead. In her defeat to see all of the red flags, she learns the consequences of her actions, but she is given the opportunity on several occasions to obey GOD. Would she finally realize that there is light at the end of the tunnel and that life can be better than she'd ever imagined? Will she ever be released from her toxic marriage? Will she gain the strength needed to move forward after all that she has endured if she just decides to trust HIM?

Portwood's goal for her readers is to know that they must have their own personal relationship with GOD and to be open and available to hear from HIM in every aspect of their life. She also wants us to know that GOD is with us in every step in our path, whether good or bad and to yield to what GOD says because day-to-day life can undoubtedly blindside us, *which may cost us*. Obey HIM and learn to embrace your trials and tribulations because the rainbow will come after the storm if you follow his command.

*The Cost of Disobedience | What price will **YOU** pay?*

*To the author of "The Cost of Disobedience,"* you epitomize elegance. Reflecting on the SHE Conference & Networking Convention, Gala No. 3, I would award you "Best Dressed" without hesitation. The event's theme was blue and gold, and you arrived in your stunning blue and gold attire, looking absolutely beautiful. Your story is a powerful testament that when we feel we can't continue on our path, God will be there to support us every step of the way.

# Dr. Calenthia Miller

**UNMASK** by Dr. Calenthia Yvette Miller | Anya finds herself between a rock and a hard place. What is she to believe, the word of a pregnant woman or the word of a person she has known for five years who grew up with Royce and knew his history of keeping company with some unsavory women? Trust a man who had no identity until tonight and whom she barely knows? Or take a chance on a person she has spent time with and has grown to admire? Can Anya resolve the issues from her past so that she will find happiness in the future?

Accommodating his need to protect and his desire to be good enough interferes with Sebastián's everyday life. He is stuck in the past. He is unable to resolve the issues stemming from his childhood. He wants to move forward and heal the pain but does not know how to take the necessary steps. Will this turmoil impact his relationship with the people he loves?

Royce is a successful attorney who has guarded his heart since losing his wife, Skylar. Trying to mask the pain, he is now potentially trapped having a baby with a woman he doesn't love. Will time reveal the truth and heal his broken heart?

Bryce has lived the life of a playboy and is now ready to settle down and be in a monogamous relationship, but he doesn't know if that is possible-until he sits across the table from a beautiful lady at a charity event. Leah is rough around the edges but determined to make it. Her relationship with Anya is closer than a sister's. She doesn't want to disappoint Anya. How far will she go to make her dreams a reality? *Will new relationships blossom out of this chaos and confusion? Only time will tell.*

*Unmask : Part II* by Dr. Calenthia Yvette Miller centers on three attractive professionals and their search for healing. Full of sensual detail and rollicking conversation, the narrative explores the lives of

Anya McMichael, Royce Blackmon, and Sebastián Collins as they cope with past traumas while trying to learn what they want from life. The protagonist is Anya, a successful executive who is forced by migraines, exhaustion, and finally, a concussion to take time for desperately needed self-care and to cope with her grief for her father. With the help of her friends and colleagues, Leah and Abbey, she begins focusing on her own needs and desires during a leave of absence. Meanwhile, she is pursued by two extremely handsome men and begins to form a daughter-like bond with an elegant dress designer who is a bereaved mother. You won't be able to put this page-turner down.

*To my sister, author of the UNMASK series*, I want you to know that we will always embody collaboration over competition. I can truly say I have a sister from another mother. Words cannot capture the depth of our relationship. I am incredibly proud of you and all you have achieved in such a short time. You have shown that even amid disappointment, blessings can shine through. What is meant for you will always be yours.

# DARION KNIGHT

*did i make you*
# PROUD

"*Did I Make You Proud*" by Darion Knight offers readers a candid and captivating look into his life journey. As a black gymnast raised in the streets of Chicago, Knight's memoir unfolds with raw honesty and authenticity. Through the release of his first book, readers are invited to delve into his narrative, tracing his evolution from inner-city struggles to entrepreneurial triumphs. Knight's inspiring memoir serves as a testament to resilience and self-determination, showcasing how he forged his own path to success against all odds. As you stay tuned for this compelling and empowering memoir, know that this read will encourage us all to cultivate a sense of inner pride and self-worth!

*To the author of Did I Make You Proud*, though our bond is through marriage, I thank you for believing in me and choosing SHE to be your publishing platform. Your faith in me has been a cornerstone of my own journey, just as I wholeheartedly believe in you and your remarkable talents. We got the opportunity to see you in a different light during those Zoom meetings when you bravely shared your story with vulnerability and authenticity.

Your family must be immensely proud of you, and rightly so. Your determination is a source of inspiration for everyone around you, myself included. You've shown me what it means to persevere, to share knowledge generously.

I look forward to our further collaboration with F.I.R.E Media, which is a true testament to your leadership and vision. Again, and as always, thank you for allowing us to share your story with the world.

# NYZIA EASTERLING

# DAN JOHNSON

EVALUATIONG COMPATIBILITY BEFORE BECOMING ONE

# 151

## QUESTIONS TO ASK
## BEFORE YOU SAY "I DO"

**151 Questions to Ask Before You Say "I Do" | Evaluating Compatibility Before Becoming One** by Dan Johnson is a guide that helps couples determine the main areas of compatibility in their relationship. Assessing your relational differences, evaluating your like-mindedness, and determining if your relationship is lasting is essential before becoming one. Be wise about choosing a suitable mate.

*To the author of "151 Questions to Ask Before You Say 'I Do',"* it was a grand introduction, and we are honored that you allowed us to publish your book. I must admit, there were questions in your manuscript that I hadn't thought to discuss with my significant other. Thank you for highlighting these important topics. We wish you all the best in your publishing journey.

# ROYCE DIXON

# hidden feelings
# REVEALED

## IS THERE MORE

***Hidden Feelings Revealed | Is There More*** by Royce Dixon Sr. is book II of the highly acclaimed series by Royce Dixon, Sr. This captivating novel delves into the lives of several attorneys whose paths intertwine amidst a gripping murder investigation. Prepare to embark on an emotional journey filled with romance, uncertainty, thrill, the pursuit of justice, and a poignant exploration of toxic masculinity. Within the pages of this compelling narrative, meet Troy, one of the central characters, as he embarks on a transformative voyage of transparency that reshapes his world in unexpected ways.

Read between the lines as this layered narrative not only entertains but also addresses vital themes, wholeheartedly supporting and advocating for domestic violence victims and the importance of mental health. So as you immerse yourself in the pages of *Hidden Feelings Revealed | Is There More,* be enthralled by its alluring storytelling, destined to capture the hearts of countless readers.

*To the distinguished leading man of SHE for 2023 and esteemed nominee and/or recipient of the Janice Anderson Author Award,*
Your presence on the cover of the BNB Newsletter mag, coupled with your extensive book tours, speaks volumes about your impact and influence within our literary community. You epitomize the essence of SHE not just by observing our actions, but by actively participating and recognizing the support and camaraderie we offer. Your stories leave lasting impressions wherever they go, showcasing our dedication to supporting and marketing our authors through initiatives like custom boxes, book banners, and our website, hence the reason you became an award-winning author on Black Authors Matter TV.

Your willingness to share your vulnerabilities and personal journey has been truly inspiring. You've shattered stereotypes and demonstrated that men have feelings too, and that they too strive to reach their fullest potential. Thank you for your contributions. We truly appreciate it.

# YOU'RE NO

## DIFFERENT THAN ME

## Martell's World
# CYNTHIA GREEN

**Martell's World : You're No Different Than Me** by Cynthia Green tells the story of a hard-of-hearing boy that feels different because of his hearing loss.

Parents and children alike will enjoy Martell's World Series, which will spark thoughtful conversations on how we are all unique but similar in many ways.

*To the author of "Martell's World,"* thank you for opening the doors to Martell's world and illuminating the experiences of the deaf community. My mother has been an instructor of American Sign Language for years and managed a building with death residents, so your work resonates deeply. It is a true blessing to learn a new way of living, which is no different than anyone else, which has been inspired by your authentic experiences.

# MARVIN MICHAEL O'BRYANT

**WHAT MY EYES HAVE SEEN, MY EARS HAVE HEARD, AND MY HEART HAS FELT**

**I Woke Up Black | What My Eyes Have Seen, My Ears Have Heard, and My Heart Has Felt by Marvin Michael O'Bryant** is a story inspired by real-life experiences. It follows the life of Marvin, who has witnessed decades of depression, poverty, and a lack of motivation in a nation struggling with love and respect. Despite these challenges, Marvin believes in the importance of respecting one another and finding value in every individual to bring out the best in society. He is deeply concerned about the persistence of racism and hopes to see a change in thinking and teaching for future generations.

Marvin's journey emphasizes the significance of sharing personal stories to inspire and support others. He encourages people to recognize that everyone has a unique narrative, and no occupation defines the worth of an individual. The central message revolves around acknowledging our shared humanity as God's children and focusing on the journey ahead, rather than dwelling on past struggles.

The book is structured to highlight racially charged events in the divided South, leading to discussions on unfair treatment. In the end, Marvin provides wisdom on regaining respect and unity to pave the way for future generations to prosper.

Ultimately, "I Woke Up Black" is a powerful testament to the truth that all humans, regardless of race, share a common purpose: to live their best lives and thrive in a world that treats them fairly and with respect.

*To the author of I Woke Up Black*, your powerful words, and the story that you have shared has challenged societal norms and sparked conversations that rippled far beyond the pages.

Working with you on this publication has been an absolute honor. I'm immensely proud to say that we serve as your publisher. Your commitment to sharing information and your desire to see SHE PUBLISHING LLC excel in the world of publishing together have been truly inspiring. Your willingness to support us in reaching higher levels, even to the extent of offering to share knowledge in your own domain, speaks volumes about your generosity and dedication.

You will forever be my brother in authorship, and someone I consider a part of my literary family.

# DESIREE A. TAYLOR

# MARK LEWIS

*Coming Soon*

# DRIVE!

## THE MOTORSPORTS ART OF
## MARK E LEWIS

# SHELITA WOODS

# MY EYES

## ANCHOR YOUR WAY TO A
## SUCCESSFUL ELDER CARE BUSINESS

**From My Eyes | Anchor Your Way to a Successful Elder Care Business** by Shelita Woods is about how to start and operate a successful elder care business. Although this book focuses on eldercare, the gems, tips, and nuggets from this book will open your eyes to any business venture you seek to accomplish. No matter what obstacles you face, degrees you have not obtained, fears of stepping out on your own, or your funding status, you can be successful if your mind's made up to succeed. This book speaks to the passion within you, setting the foundation, do's and don'ts regarding the operations, and the personal touch every establishment needs. You will learn about the ends and outs of how to run the elder care business and components that may not be taught in any annual classroom. So many successful entrepreneurs are unwilling to share how they have become successful, but Woods is here to share every step of my journey with you.

That said, it's time for you to dream, write it down, put things into motion, and go for it. If you stumble, get on your feet and keep moving. Let no one stop your vision. Be the fly on the wall as Woods take you through her journey, as she tells all, *From My Eyes*.

*To the author of From My Eyes*, I want to take a moment to express my sincere gratitude for you writing this insightful book. Your work not only provides invaluable guidance on starting and operating an elder care business but also offers universal principles that can be applied to any entrepreneurial endeavor.

Your book is a treasure of wisdom, filled with gems, tips, and nuggets that open our eyes to the possibilities of success, regardless of the obstacles we may face or the conventional paths we may not have followed.

In a world where many successful entrepreneurs guard their secrets closely, your openness and willingness to guide others on their path to success are refreshing and deeply appreciated.

# RICHNOVATED

**E.N.G.I.N.E.E.R. Your Way** by RICHNOVATED is a memoir that shares the author's personal journey! Drawing from his own experiences as an engineer, RICHNOVATED shares valuable insights and life lessons that are applicable to individuals from all walks of life, encompassing not only his journey from childhood to becoming a technical professional but also his ventures as an entrepreneur and community leader.

This book offers valuable insights and life lessons applicable to anyone seeking excellence in technical roles, entrepreneurship, or personal growth. Richnovated provides a blueprint for embracing opportunities, navigating challenges, fostering innovation, and nurturing relationships. Although centered around engineering, the wisdom goes beyond the technical realm.

Filled with inspiring quotes from prominent STEM leaders, educators, and successful business owners, this book serves as a powerful tool to help readers unlock their full potential and achieve greatness in all aspects of their lives, whether it be personal or professional.

*To the author of ENGINEER YOUR WAY*, I extend my heartfelt gratitude for your collaboration with us and for hosting a branding session for the SheFamily. I'll also always remember our introduction in Houston, Texas. You've become a true brother to me in the world of authorship.

I'm inspired by your willingness to share information and insights with me, even when we were initially strangers. Your actions were genuine and heartfelt.

About a year later, you graciously allowed us to publish your story, and since then, every individual you've referred to our company has exhibited the same level of excellence as you. Your professionalism is exemplary. Hearing about your journey, from having a low GPA to achieving such remarkable success, is truly inspiring. Despite your immense following, you remain humble in all your endeavors.

# SHADOW

## OF RETRIBUTION

# KAMRIN

"*Shadow of Retribution*" by Kamrin follows the harrowing journey of Bruce Butler Andrews, a former MMA fighter, English teacher, and ex-special forces member whose life is shattered when he becomes the target of a vengeful cartel. After his encounter with the cartel, Bruce finds himself relentlessly pursued, culminating in a brutal attack on his home where he is left unconscious.

Upon awakening and despite the overwhelming despair, Bruce finds within himself a renewed determination to seek justice and protect his loved ones. As he stands amidst the wreckage of the battle, he knows that his journey is far from over. His resolve is unwavering, fueled by his love for his family and the desire for retribution against those who have wronged them.

As readers reflect on Bruce's tumultuous journey, one question lingers: What fate awaits Andrew as he stands at the crossroads of life and death, driven by love and a thirst for justice?

*To the author of Shadow of Retribution*, you will be the inspiration for many boys and girls. Keep up the great work.

# DANIELLE BROWN

## I LUV ME

**"I Luv Me"** a National Daughters Day release by Danielle Brown is a captivating poetry book aimed at cultivating self-esteem and confidence in children. It explores essential themes such as the significance of relationships, the power of community, and the appreciation of nature and the environment. These elements profoundly influence our personal journeys and overall well-being. The book imparts valuable lessons on self-love, the importance of connections, and an appreciation for the world around us. Readers will discover that embracing their true selves and valuing the people and things in their lives greatly contribute to their quality of life.

The poetry book commences with verses dedicated to loving and appreciating one's physical appearance, family, and friendships. The inclusion of vibrant illustrations enhances the poetic experience, igniting the imagination of each child. Furthermore, every 2-3 poems are accompanied by assessment pages featuring insightful questions, as well as activity pages that encourage children to express themselves creatively.

Danielle Brown strives to convey to her readers that trials and challenges are an inevitable part of life, even in adulthood. However, when one's core values are fortified and self-love remains at the center, no valley is insurmountable, and no mountain is too high to climb. Unconditional self-belief and self-love, embracing both strengths and imperfections, serve as the bedrock for overcoming life's obstacles.

*To the author of "I Luv Me,"* your book will build the self-esteem and confidence for children everywhere. Your poetry's focus on the significance of relationships, community, and the environment is both timely and timeless. I am proud of you. It was great to reconnect with you as you attended the marketing session with Richnovated, your brother in authorship, as he presented "The Six Sauces of Branding." Keep moving forward because you can do it!

# DR. SAMUEL I. BROWN

*wounds can heal*
## EVEN IF SCARS
REMAIN

*"Wounds Can Heal: Even if Scars Remain | Healing Emotional Wounds Through the Power of Forgiveness"* by Samuel I. Brown is a compelling exploration of the transformative power of forgiveness in the journey toward healing. This enlightening book exposes the destructive nature of harboring unforgiveness and its impediment to personal growth. It offers a roadmap to inner peace and emphasizes that healing is attainable regardless of the depth or duration of one's wounds.

The book underscores the importance of self-awareness, encouraging readers to confront the sources of their pain and challenge their self-limiting beliefs. Rather than remaining trapped in cycles of anger and blame, it advocates for the liberation that forgiveness can bring.

Drawing connections to self-care, resilience, trauma recovery, mental health, emotional well-being, self-love, and acceptance, *"Wounds Can Heal: Even if Scars Remain"* explores the intricate web of emotions that shape our lives. It stresses the significance of effective communication, nurturing healthy relationships, and empowering oneself as essential components of the forgiveness and healing process.

Throughout the book, readers are guided through a range of emotional wounds and shown how understanding, acceptance, and forgiveness, both for oneself and others, can lead to profound healing. It provides practical advice for dealing with emotions such as guilt, anger, bitterness, and resentment, illuminating the path to greater empathy, compassion, and overall well-being.

The key message of *"Wounds Can Heal: Even if Scars Remain"* is a powerful one: it is never too late to find healing, acceptance, and peace in our lives. Through self-reflection, forgiveness, and compassion—for both ourselves and others—we can break free from the shackles of our past and embrace a future marked by newfound freedom and emotional liberation. This book serves as a guiding light for anyone seeking a more fulfilling and harmonious life.

*To the author of Wounds Can Heal Even if Scars Remain*, we extend our heartfelt gratitude for your invaluable contributions to the SHE family. You not only prioritize yourself but also consider the needs of others. Despite facing the loss of your father during this process, causing a delay in the publication of your book, your determination remained unwavering.

Your initiative in seeking additional support led to the creation of an author orientation for writers across the sister companies. This included the development of materials such as a PowerPoint presentation and updates to our SHE WRITERS PLANNER.

Since then, you've consistently shared your wealth of ideas with us, emphasizing the importance of collaboration and support in achieving success. Your commitment to treating us like family has blossomed into a true alliance.

# ALICIA MOORE

# MARC A. BEAUSEJOUR

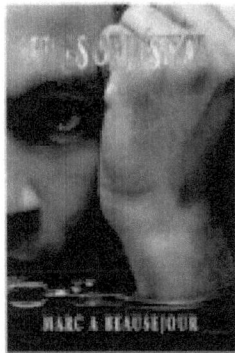

*the Black Cyrano*
## SERIES

**The BlackCyrano Series** by Marc A. Beausejour

**DIVINE VENGEANCE** | After the murder of David Anderson, LaToya Richardson awaits her day in court while attorney Edward Reed receives a warning from Tadarius Hill, the gang leader of M.O.B. and sexy femme fatale Tina, who gives him an ultimatum. Can Edward Chris, and Andrea summon the strength amidst the chaos in their environment to secure their futures?

**THE PREACHER'S WEB** | The pages of "The Preacher's Web" beckon you to explore the complexities of morality and redemption. Can Mike Hillman rise above, or will he be consumed by the web of his past?

**ADIA'S BALLAD** | With fame corrupting her relationships with those she loves, will Andrea aka Adia find the inner peace and closure she seeks, or will she succumb to the draw of money and celebrity?

**FIRES OF JUSTICE** | "The controversies confronted, stirred, and then addressed in this story have no choice but to awaken you to new perspectives that might not have ever crossed your mind. Readers, all I can say is be prepared to feel the fire that Beausejour has ignited in this suspenseful masterpiece!"

—D.A. Goodwin, author of The Offender I Once Defended

**SPLIT DECISION** | Prepare to enter the ring as cultures clash in this adrenaline-filled drama! With a fight against the undefeated Dominican champion Felipe Maximo looming, secrets are revealed, and friends turn to foes as Sylvio later discovers that he may not be fighting only for the middleweight crown, but he may also be fighting for his life.

**SPLIT DECISION 2: The Comeback** | As he prepares for his toughest ring battle yet, can Sylvio and Jim find the fortitude to emerge victorious while putting all their struggles behind them?

**STREET RETRIBUTION** | New York City attorney Edward Reed harbors a secret. Will Edward and David survive the bounty, or will they fall victim to the code of the streets?

*To the author of the BlackCyrano series*, we are immensely grateful for the chance to collaborate and contribute to making black history alongside SHE PUBLISHING LLC. Your achievements have earned you the cover spot on the February BNB Newsletter Mag, highlighting the significant strides you've made through hard work, dedication, appreciation, and the efforts that you make on a daily basis. With the launch of six books on our roster, each day of the week starting from Monday, February 19, 2024, your impact will be felt far and wide. I foresee a move on the rise, so let's speak that into existence. My favorite quote is speaking what you seek until you see what you've said. Thank you for embracing this transition and placing your trust in us! We look forward to many more milestones together and are excited to see where this journey takes us next.

# VITINA WILLIS

"CRACKING THE CODE | 10 POSSIBLE REASONS YOU DIDN'T GET THE JOB"

*Bobby*

# MCNEIL JR.

CRACKING THE CODE

**Latoya**

# JOHNSON

## THE BEAUTY BENEATH

MINDS
MINES

-------------

A

POETRY

COLLECTION

OF

HER-STORY

"THE ACT OF LOVE, CARING, AND NOT QUITTING"

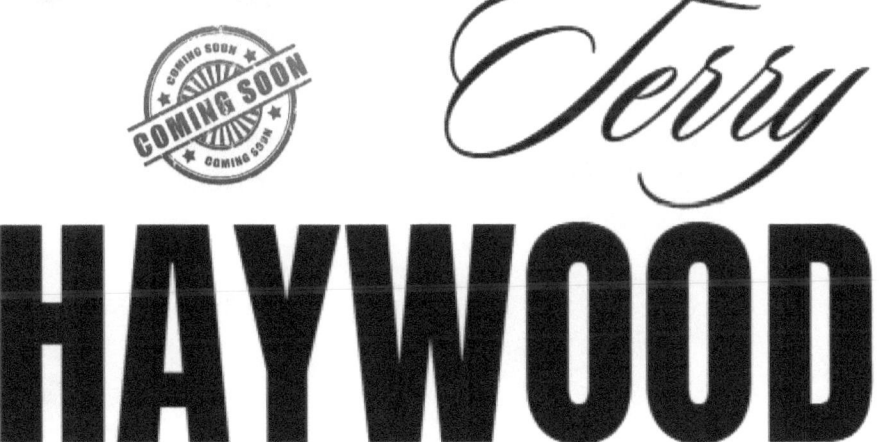

# ECHO'S TALE

## THE BURDEN OF
## THE TALE

# Khanyon G. Jerome

**Echo's Tale : Burden Of The Tale** by Khanyon G. Jerome | In the city of Wallacgrum, located in the middle of the country of Railam, known for its beautiful meadows and cherry blossom trees, is a place where the great King Fayos shone his benevolent light upon all his people. However, all that changed when the king fell ill and began having ridiculous dreams about the tail of a dragon that can cure anything. As desperate as the king was, his insanity drove him to mandate the whole kingdom to find this tail. However, a young Nubian man named Koldiar and three foolish men intercepted his royal decree and set off to steal this supernatural tail.

This story follows Koldiar as he treks through uncomfortable situations and unfortunate events to become the king's holy knight and to find his faith, but despite his goal, he soon finds love in a caramel-skinned woman with diamond-blue eyes named Echo, who will be forced to choose between a love so pure and a love of guilt.

Through this journey, Koldiar must be exceptionally careful with Echo, as winning her love is not an easy task because Koldiar would soon find out...she is the tail of old, the tail brightened, the dragon of the blue flame! She is Echo, and this is her tale! Or is it?

*To the author of Echo's Tale*, the moment we met you and your family, it became evident that there was something truly special about you guys. Your presence at the National Black Book Festival in Houston, TX marked by an artful excellence set you apart. Your characters came to life, as they gracefully walked through the event and captivating the attention of the attendees. Because of this, and your determination to succeed, you have graced the cover of the BNB Newsletter Mag!!! In addition, we congratulate you on your new bundle of joy.

# The Family Operation:
## The Backbone of the Dream

Beyond the spotlight, a dedicated team worked to transform dreams into tangible realities. Mama*She*, Chrissy, J. Camille, J. Alexis, J. Alexandria, J. Lynniece, Sir Caleb, the Elite Editing Team and later T. Frecker, Cynthia, and Sahara – each a force of nature, weaving their own magic behind the curtains. All of these people taught me the power of collaboration, the significance of support, and the unyielding spirit that makes impossible, possible.

Together, we built a haven for creativity, a space where vulnerability was met with understanding, and where dreams were nurtured into blossoming realities. Each late-night session, each brainstorming meeting, each hurdle overcome, stands as a testament to the strength we found in the community. Thank you, dear team, for being the backbone of SHE Publishing LLC, the silent heroes who brought this symphony of voices to life.

# EPILOGUE

## TURNING THE FINAL PAGES

*A Glimpse into Our Future*

*"The Author & Publisher, a voice born from the echoes of SHE Publishing."* –Shenitha Finesse Anniece

As I close this story, I do so with a heart overflowing with gratitude. To the authors, the team, the readers, and the universe that conspired to bring this dream to life – thank you. Thank you for the sleepless nights fueled by passion, the moments of doubt silenced by belief, and the joy of witnessing words transform into wings, carrying dreams to unimaginable heights.

Dive into the world of SHE Publishing LLC, where stories empower and voices resonate, and if you are ready to embark on a journey of inspiration, connection, and empowerment, look no further than the SHE Publishing LLC family! Our platform is a vibrant community where authors support each other, they share their diverse experiences, perspectives, and triumphs with the world.

Visit our website at www.shepublishingllc.com to discover a treasure of captivating reads from talented authors who are breaking barriers and redefining narratives. Connect with these incredible storytellers, engage with their work, and be part of the conversation that's shaping the future.

But wait, there's more! We invite you to share your own stories with us. Your voice matters, and we're passionate about providing a platform for every voice to be heard. Whether it's through personal essays, memoir, poetry, children, or fiction, your story has the power to inspire and uplift others.

Exciting things are on the horizon for SHE Publishing LLC! We're gearing up for something special, where we are marketing our authors on another level. You can find exclusive merchandise on our platforms, and feel free to support your favorite authors. Plus, we're onboarding an even more talented group of authors and writers, who will represent the class of 2024| the underground leads for you to explore or be a part of.

And that's not all – you will continue seeing our authors grace the covers of the prestigious BNB newsletter mag, captivating readers worldwide. Picture book tours that bring these remarkable authors to communities near and far, spreading their messages of hope and resilience.

But perhaps the most thrilling development yet to be untold. We can't tell it all. Be on the lookout for *From Projects to Publisher | Part II* and you shall see what's come to fruition!

So, are you ready to be part of something extraordinary? Join us on this incredible journey. Stay tuned for the exciting adventures yet to come, and together, we will shape a future where every voice is heard, and every story matters.

Remember, you are not just a reader; you are a storyteller. Turn the page, write your legacy, and inspire the world. Let our symphony of voices continue, each page a note, each story a verse, in this grand composition of life.

This isn't goodbye, but a "see you soon," for the pages never truly end. They fold, they unfold, they metamorphose into new chapters, new journeys, new stories waiting to be told. So, take this torch, embrace the fire in your soul, and write your own epic story. The world awaits your unique voice, your authentic truth, your masterpiece waiting to be written. *Write the story you want to read; better yet, write the story you want to live.*

PUBLISH | SELL | SHOP with
SHE PUBLISHING LLC
www.shepublishingllc.com
T: 219.515.8032

Everybody has a story to tell.
Share Your Story with the World!

# GALLERY:

## WRITE THE STORY

*You Want to Live*

---Shenitha Finesse Anniece

# *author* ASPIRATIONS

❝ As an author, one of my goals is to get my work into the hands of more readers. One of the strategies I've decided to pursue is being more visible at vendor events. These events are great opportunities to connect with book lovers face to face, share my work, and build a community of readers who are interested in what I have to offer. This is the only way to ensure that my work is seen and appreciated by those who will genuinely enjoy it.

DR. CALENTHIA MILLER

VISIT WWW.SHEPUBLISHINGLLC.COM

# *author* EPIGRAPH

❝ The rain and thunder aroused Anya from her sleep. The beautiful views of the Atlantic Ocean were replaced by massive waves that appeared to be angry. She massaged her aching temples, praying that the pain would go away.

UNMASK | UNCOVERING THE TRUTH

VISIT WWW.SHEPUBLISHINGLLC.COM

# *author* EPIGRAPH

❝ Remember, you are not just a writer, you are a storyteller. Turn the page, write your legacy, and inspire the world.

FROM PROJECTS TO PUBLISHER

VISIT WWW.SHEPUBLISHINGLLC.COM

# *author* ASPIRATIONS

❝ My goal is to be more active with my book in a sense of social and media presence. It's always been a little scary to put myself and my book out there, but I am proud of my work, so I think it deserves to be seen.

AUTHOR OF ECHO'S TALE
BURDEN OF THE TALE
by Khamo G. Jones

VISIT WWW.SHEPUBLISHINGLLC.COM

## SEASON IV
# SHEPUB NETWORK

Thurs. Feb. 29th at 7:30 PM CST/8:30 PM EST

### with Shenitha Finesse & S.R. Mays

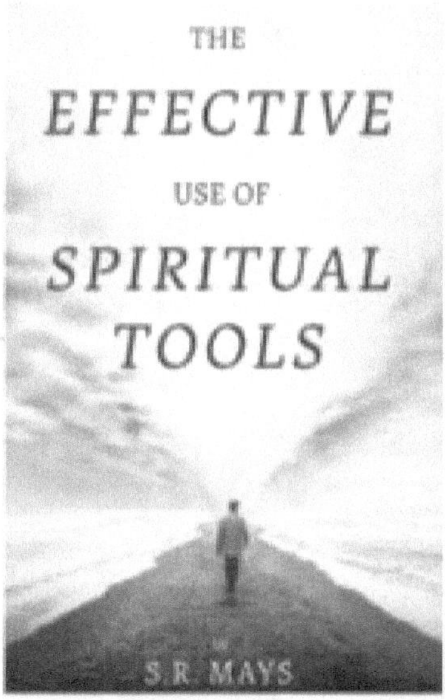

THE
*EFFECTIVE*
USE OF
*SPIRITUAL*
*TOOLS*

by S.R. MAYS

PUBLISH | SELL | SHOP

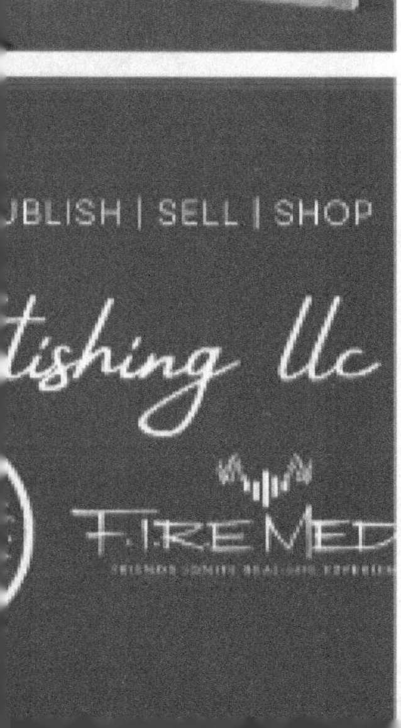

*...tishing llc*

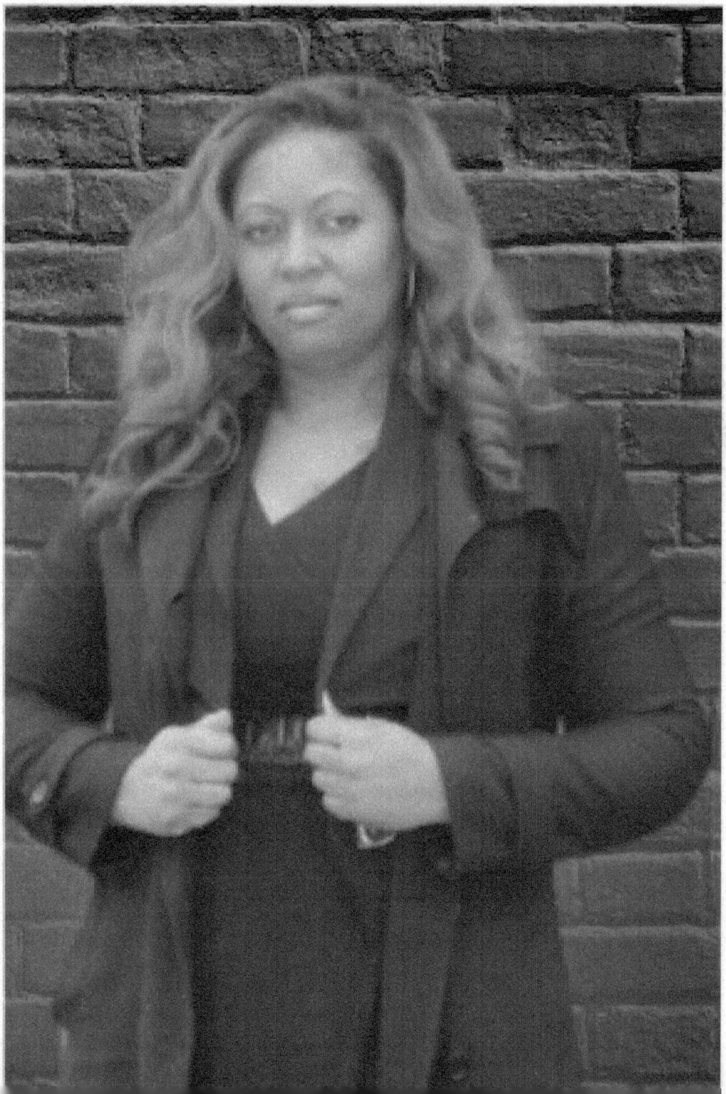

FIRE MED

YOU'RE
NO
Than
ME

WORLD
YOU'RE
NO
Than
ME

YOU'RE

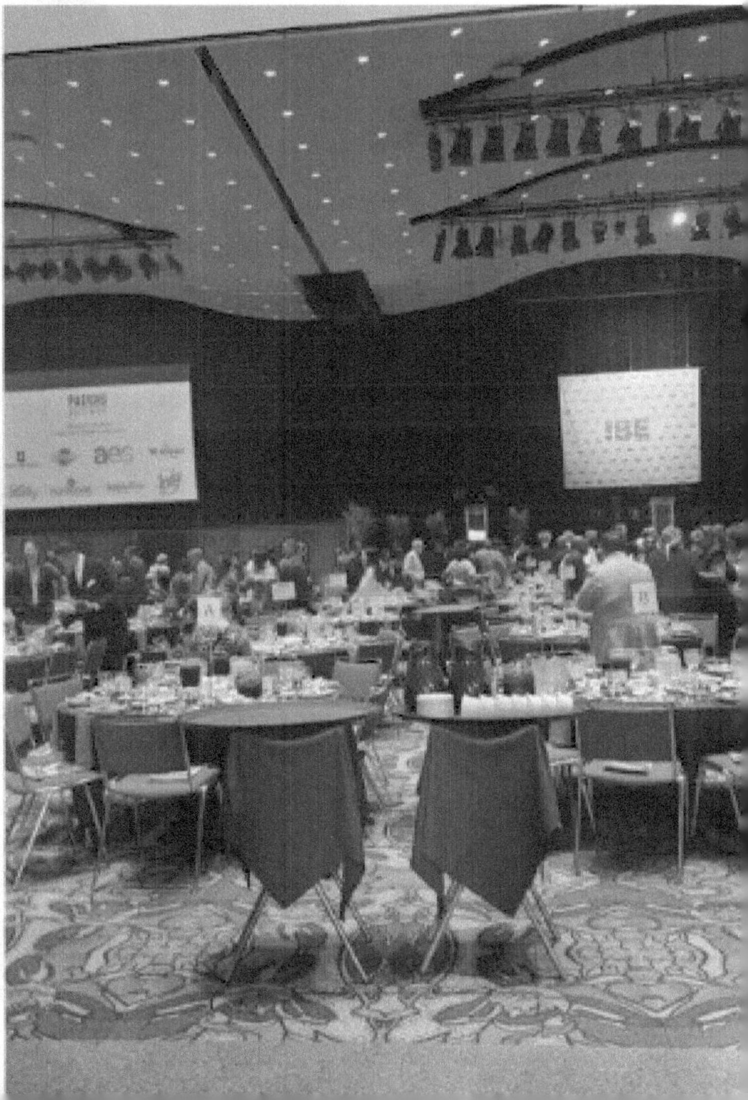
aes
IBE

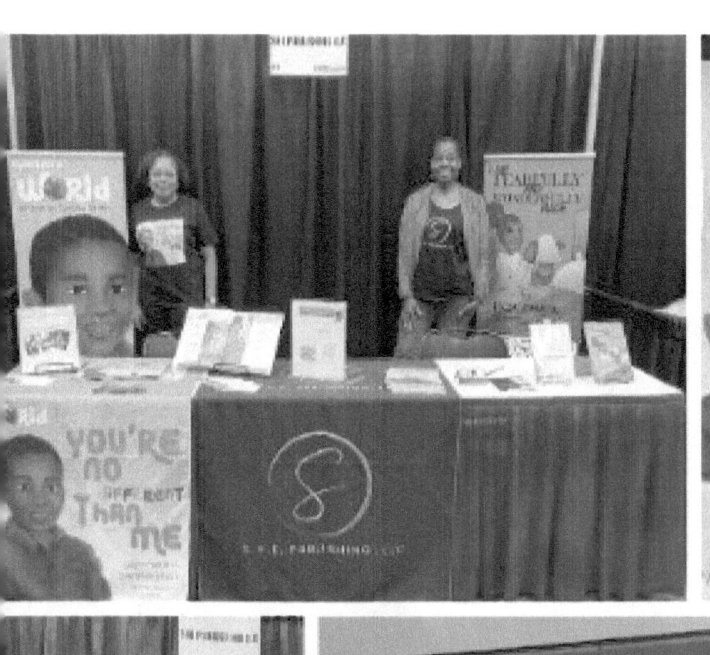

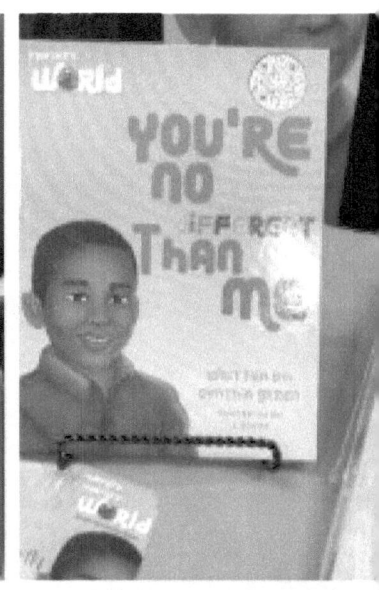

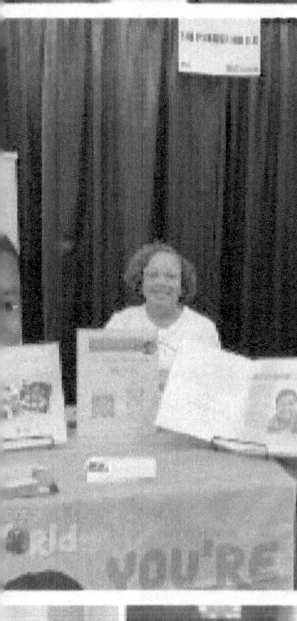

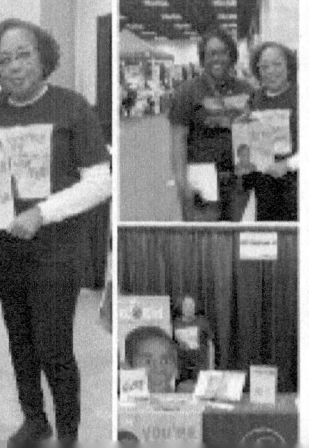

THE SHE
PUBLISHING
FAMILY
GALLERY
2020-23

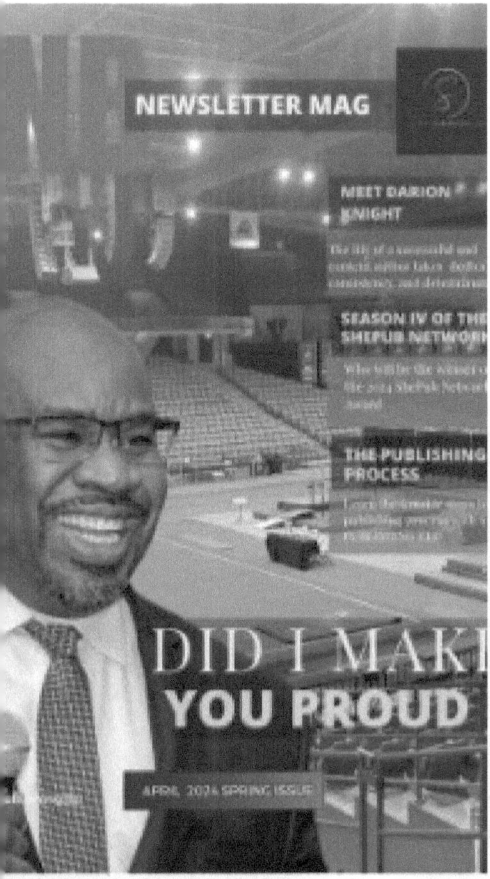
NEWSLETTER MAG
MEET DARION KNIGHT
SEASON IV OF THE SHEPUB NETWORK
THE PUBLISHING PROCESS
DID I MAKE
YOU PROUD
APRIL 2024 SPRING ISSUE

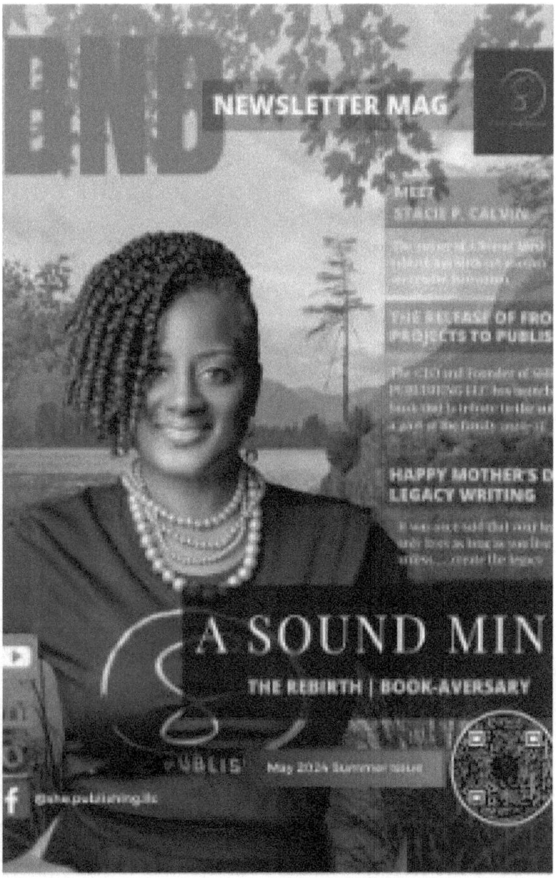
BNB
NEWSLETTER MAG
MEET STACIE P. CALVIN
HAPPY MOTHER'S DAY LEGACY WRITING
A SOUND MIN
THE REBIRTH | BOOK-AVERSARY
May 2024 Summer Issue
@she.publishing.llc

NEWSLETTER MAG
MEET AUTHOR CYNTHIA GREEN
AMERICAN SIGN LANGUAGE
SHE PUBLISHING LLC GOES GLOBAL
WOMEN'S
HER-STORY MONTH

BNB
NEWSLETTER MAG
BREAKING BOUNDARIES
TOP 5 AUTHOR SERVICES
FROM PROJECTS TO PUBLISHER
NEW YEAR
THE MASTERFUL MARKETING MAVEN
- THE PUBLICIST -

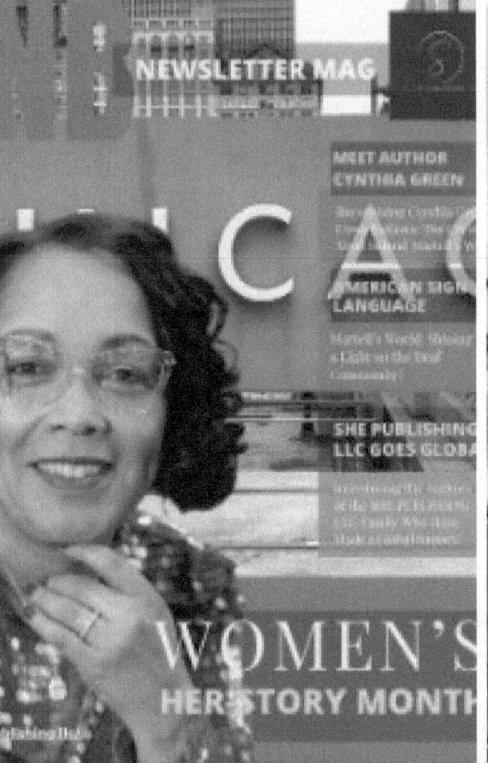

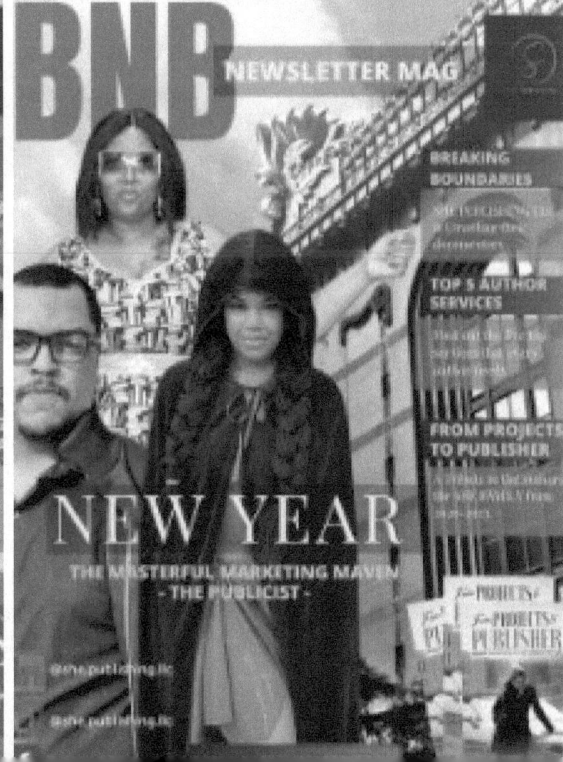

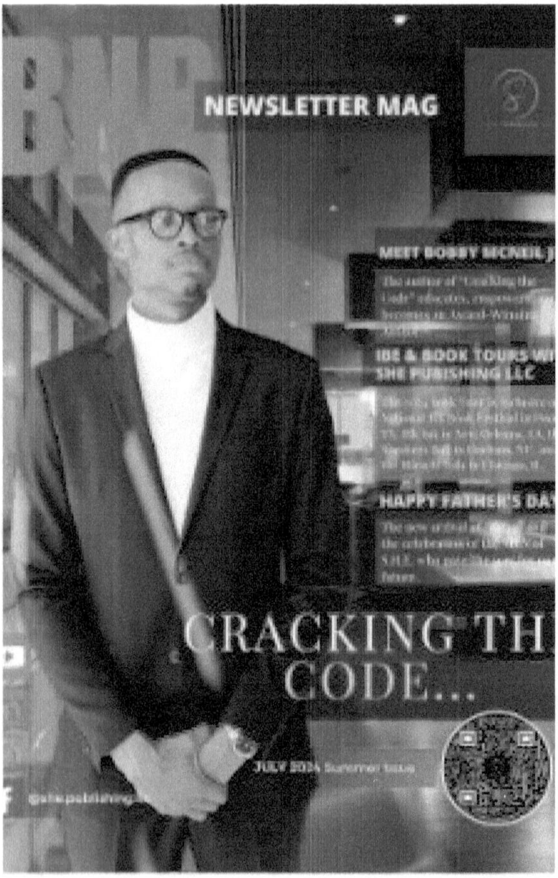
NEWSLETTER MAG
MEET BOBBY MCNEIL J
IBE & BOOK TOURS WI
SHE PUBISHING LLC
HAPPY FATHER'S DAY
CRACKING TH
CODE...
JULY 2024 Summer Issue

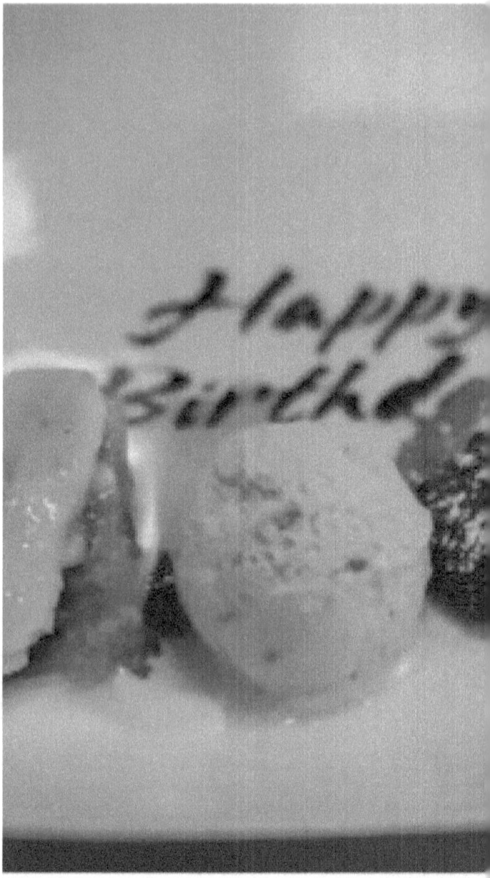

THE WHITE HOUSE

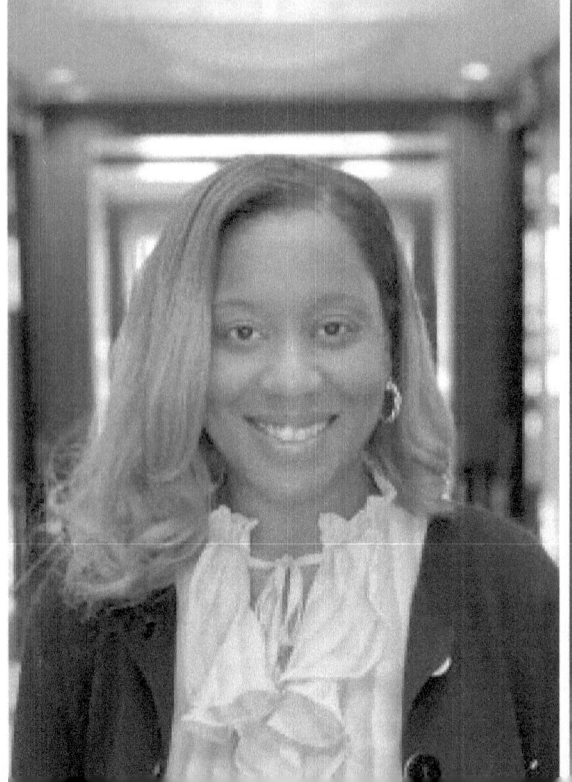

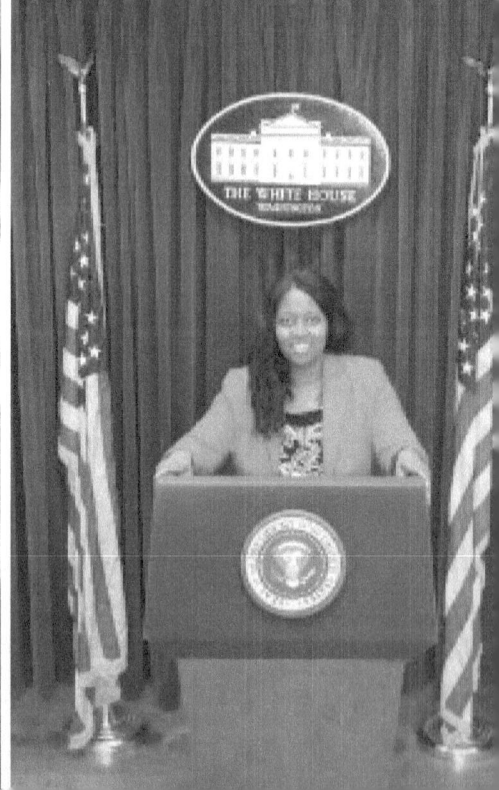

Happy

BLK INK BC
FESTIVAL
Author Exhibitor
AUTHOR
MARC
BEAUSEJOUR

LK INK BO
ESTIVAL
Author Exhibitor

LK INK BO
ESTIVAL
Author Exhibitor

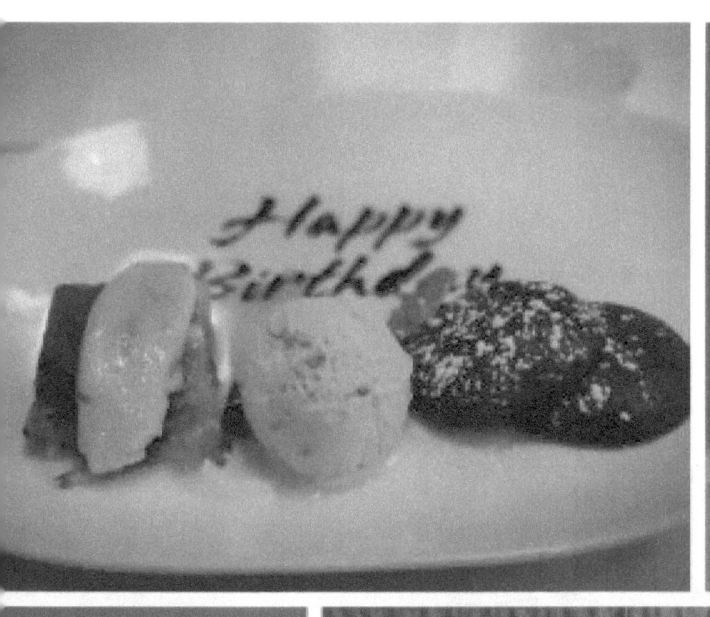

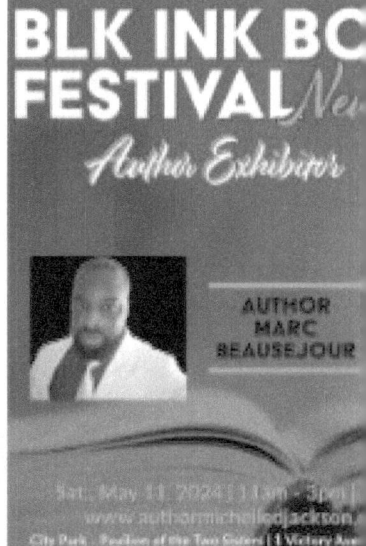

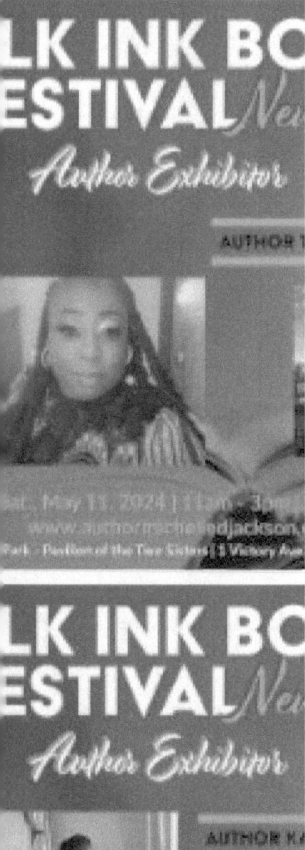

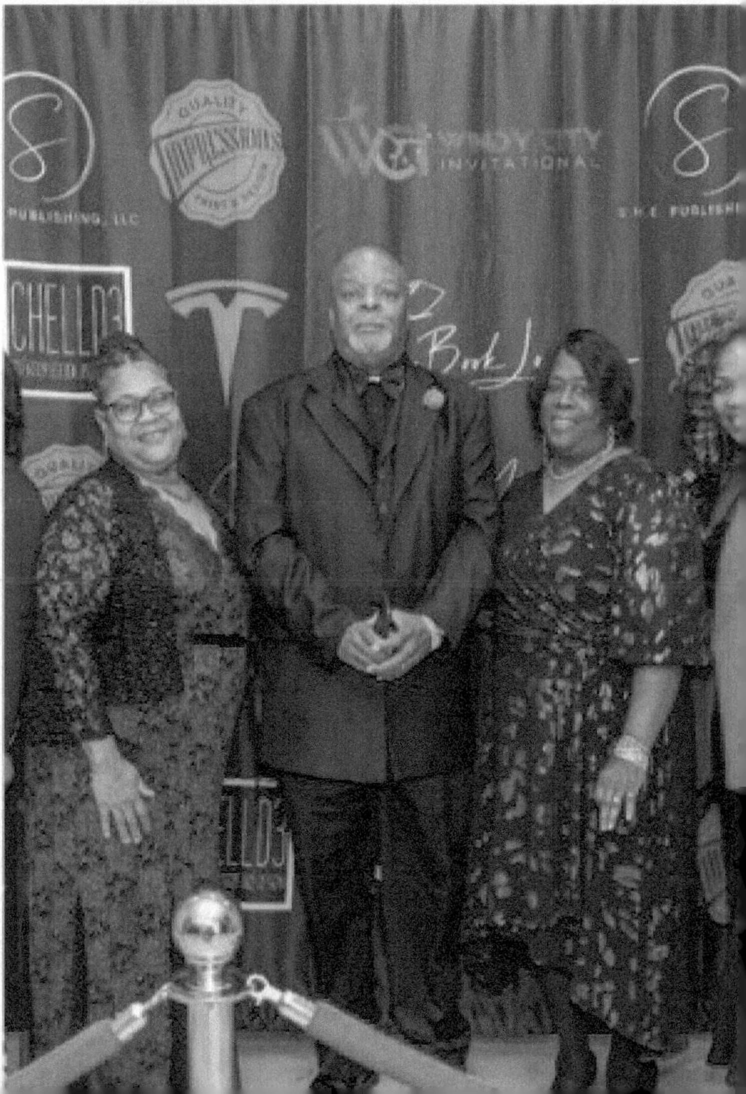
INVITATIONAL

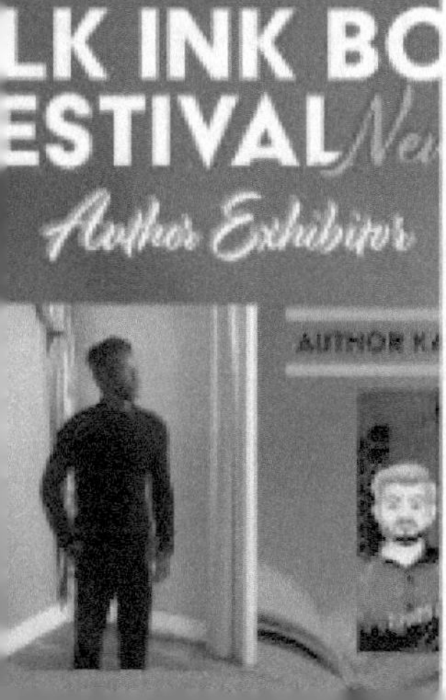

Superhero

Jordyn's Juvenilia

Shadow of Retribution

KAMRIN

I AM
FEARFULLY
AND♥
WONDERFULLY
MADE

♥        ♥

♥

Licia Johnson

WORLD

YOU'RE
NO
DIFFERENT
THAN
ME

WRITTEN BY
SHENA BROWN

5 Jordyn's Juvenilia

D

DETHROUGHT

BY DANIELLE BROWN

SHENITHA FIRESSE ANNIECE

# NATURE'S
## *Alure*

### SECRETS OF ATTRACTION:
#### THE PUPPET MASTER'S DANCE

# TRANSPARENCY

NENE MORRIS

# BOUNDARIES

*Evita Howard*

SHENITHA BURTON

# Forgiveness

rise and grind

AMAZING

SHE
MOOD

CHELLO3
BIG TSU

QUALITY
IMPRESSIONS
S.H.E. PUBLISHING, LLC
WINDY CITY
INVITATIONAL
CHELLO3
Book Lounge
Writer
WHEELZ
Making my spirit smile

I love you

warm

fall

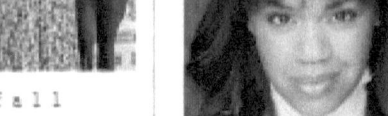

cozy

authentic

slow

Shenitha Finesse

# First Impressions Matter

**elegant**

**fashion**

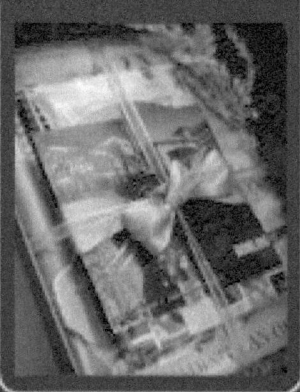

**inspiration**

**beauty**

**tenderness**

**style**

**femininity**

**relax**

**aesthetics**

# PRAISE FOR *SEEKING SHAMA*

"Need a ride to Peace and Love? Kee Kee Buckley and her trusty navigator Yoda have saved you a seat. As someone who came of age in the Age of Aquarius when everybody and his soul brother was trying to find enlightenment and the road was the metaphor, I'm impressed by how fearlessly and often poetically Buckley has taken her very personal and bracingly intimate affirmation and created something much bigger, profound and universal."

— **Ernest Thompson, Academy Award-winning screenwriter of**
*On Golden Pond* **and author of** *The Book of Maps*

"*Seeking Shama* is more than a road trip; it's a raw, brave, and beautifully told story of falling apart and finding your way back to wholeness. Through grief, heartbreak, and healing, Kee Kee invites us into her search for peace with vulnerability, humor, and so much heart. I laughed, I cried, and I saw pieces of myself on every page."

— **Kim Goldman, Two-time** *New York Times*
**bestselling author and victims' rights advocate**

"*Seeking Shama* isn't just a story—it's a blueprint for waking up. Kee Kee Buckley ditches the success script, hits the road with her dog, and rebuilds life from the inside out. This book shows you how to turn burnout into breakthrough and heartbreak into horsepower. If you're ready to stop performing and start aligning, *Seeking Shama* delivers the roadmap."

— **Dave Asprey, Creator of biohacking,**
*New York Times* **special author**

"*Seeking Shama* is a soulful and sharply honest memoir about losing it all—and finding something even better."

— **Brad Warner, Zen monk and author of**
*Hardcore Zen* **and** *The Other Side of Nothing*

"Kee Kee has given us a beautiful story filled with courage and possibility. Her authentic, intimate writing is a balm to the soul and an inspiration to move us forward to fulfill our potential and trust our inner compass to guide us in our journey to fulfillment."

— Agapi Stassinopoulos, Author of *Speaking with Spirit* and *Wake Up to the Joy of You*

"A delightful, thought-provoking memoir about the adventure of change. This book will surely inspire others to summon curiosity and courage when facing their own crossroads. Thank you, Kee Kee, for bringing us along on your journey."

— Dr. Susan Biali, MD, Expert in stress resilience and burnout prevention, author of *The Resilient Life* and *Live a Life You Love*